Muslims under non-Muslim Rule

IBN TAYMIYYA

MUSLIMS UNDER NON-MUSLIM RULE

IBN TAYMIYYA

on
fleeing from sin; kinds of emigration;
the status of Mardin: domain of peace/war,
domain composite; the conditions
for challenging power

Texts translated, annotated and presented in relation to six modern readings of the Mardin fatwa

by

YAHYA MICHOT

Foreword by JAMES PISCATORI

Interface Publications

Published by

INTERFACE PUBLICATIONS

Oxford • London

Interface Publications
15 Rogers Street
Oxford. OX2 7JS

Company address:
2nd floor 145–157 St John St.
London. EC1V 4PY

http//interfacepublications.com

ISBN-10: 0–9554545–0–6
ISBN-13: 978–0–9554545–6–1

Typeset in Garamond, 11.5/15

Printed in Turkey by Mega Basım Yayın San. ve Tic. A.Ş.
Çobançeşme Ma. Kalender Sok. No: 9 3530 Yenibosna.
Istanbul.
e: export@mega.com.tr

PUBLISHER'S NOTE

This book was originally written in French and published by Les Éditions Albouraq as no. 4 in their series 'Fetwas d'Ibn Taymiyya': Y. MICHOT, *IBN TAYMIYYA, Mardin: Hégire, fuite du péché et demeure de l'Islam* (Beirut, 2004). This text, with the incorporation of a number of minor corrections and additions by the author, was translated into English by Jamil Qureshi, then checked over by Yahya Michot. The *Chronology* appended to this English edition (as before: translated by J. Qureshi, checked by Y. Michot, with minor corrections and updating of information) first appeared as *Le Shaykh de l'Islam Ibn Taymiyya: chronique d'une vie de théologien militant* in Y. MICHOT, *IBN TAYMIYYA, Les intermédiaires entre Dieu et l'homme* (Paris: AEIF, 1996), 21–27.

YAHYA MICHOT: Lecturer in Islamic theology, theology faculty, University of Oxford, fellow at the Oxford Centre for Islamic Studies. One of the Western world's leading authorities on Islamic philosophy and theology, especially Avicenna and Ibn Taymiyya.

JAMES PISCATORI: Lecturer in politics and international relations, social studies faculty, University of Oxford, fellow at Wadham College and the Oxford Centre for Islamic Studies. A leading authority on the Middle East, especially modern and contemporary reform and revival movements.

CONTENTS

List of Illustrations

AUTHOR'S PREFACE TO THIS EDITION

November 30th, 2007/Dhū l-Qaʿda 20, 1428 will be the 700th anniversary of the death of Ibn Taymiyya in a prison cell of the citadel of Damascus. Should we look forward to academic conferences, scholarly publications, or other commemoration of the great man's life and work? Given that, in what was once the Cemetery of the Sufis[1] in the Syrian capital, the very headstone of the Shaykh al-Islām's grave is cracked and has been left unrepaired, with fragments of it lying about on the ground, we should probably not expect too much...

The fact is, this great Mamlūk theologian continues to be presented, unjustly, as an extremist, with many dire, radical positions attached to his name. That image of him is a grave distortion. My modest hope for the present work is that, by showing how far his ideas have been misunderstood – as much, often enough, by Muslims as by non-Muslims – the texts and arguments in it may contribute to correcting the injustice done to his name.

---

1 Ibn Taymiyya's grave is all that survives of this Cemetery, razed by the French colonial authorities (1920–46) to make way for a modern hospital. For how this one grave came to be saved, and reflections on its present state, see MICHOT, *Pour une tombe.*

Of far wider importance than such rehabilitation of one of Islam's greatest medieval scholars are the questions raised in this work about relations between Muslims and the rest of the world, about Muslim presence and potential in a non-Muslim socio-political setting. Hence the title for this English edition. The various Taymiyyan texts translated will show that such presence and its rules and modalities are more complex than is assumed – especially by those who claim that Islam's Prophet came with nothing but violence and inhumanity, and so reinforce the call for new crusades to save 'civilization' from a so-called 'Islamic threat'.

Like most of my translations of Ibn Taymiyya's writings, this book was originally published in French. Credit for the English version is due to Dr. Jamil Qureshi, who initiated the project, conscientiously translated the entire work, and looked after the publishing process. I am indeed most grateful for his diligence and the unusual combination of skills he has brought to the task. That said, any deficiencies or shortcomings that remain in the work are due to me.

Yahya Michot
Oxford
Ramaḍān 1427/October 2006

FOREWORD

Islamism, though one of the defining features of the present time, remains poorly understood and, often, deliberately misinterpreted. Many see in it a decisive threat to Western civilization or, at the least, to its political hegemony. At times it has also been judged as being manipulable by regimes in Muslim countries and a convenient cover for them. The Islamists see themselves as inheritors of a long, uninterrupted tradition and present themselves as defenders of the faith, even as the articulators of 'Islam'. In this powerful and original work, Yahya Michot mines his formidable knowledge of medieval Islamic thought to clarify the modern discussion and question the conventional wisdom.

There are some fundamental principles that inspire Muslim societies across boundaries of time and culture. Nevertheless, the invention of tradition is also a constant temptation for believers, as indeed for outside observers. Nowhere is this more clearly visible than in the widespread allegation that Ibn Taymiyya is the torchbearer of dissent, precursor of the Islamic revolutionaries of today. The supposed radicals make show of following the injunctions of the great Shaykh to resist non-Islamic rulers; and some commentators join with them in routinely invoking his formal opinion as justification for anti-regime activity. As Yahya Michot convincingly argues, an examination of the sources, stripped of emotion, reveals a far more nuanced perspective. Ibn Taymiyya's concern, vis-à-vis the presence of the Mongols in the south-east of Turkey, had for its particular object the invasion of the Islamic *umma* by foreign, non-Islamic forces. In point of fact, the 'enemy within' was not his fight; the duty to resist invaders was.

The terms in which Ibn Taymiyya formulates the discussion recur extensively in the modern political vocabulary. Did the Mongol occupation of Mardin some seven centuries ago place it beyond the domain of Islam and, that being so, did this necessitate the emigration (*hijra*) of the believers? The same sort of questions hold the attention of many authors today, from Palestine and Saudi Arabia to South Asia and Indonesia. The exact terms may vary from place to place but the same bifurcation – of *Islamic* as against *non-Islamic* – resonates across all the debates and fires Muslim political controversy.

The epoch of imperialism gave a renewed urgency to the matter. For example, in 1841, a little after General Bugeaud had arrived to take command of the French troops in Algeria, his aides convinced him to try and get a fatwa that would legitimize French domination. This legitimization was the more important as the local emir, ʿAbd al-Qādir, the leader of a jihād against the French, had declared that the Muslims must not submit to unbelieving rulers, and that Muslims who helped them and served as their accomplices themselves became unbelievers. He had obtained a fatwa to this effect from the ulema of Fez. The French, with the encouragement of the emir's rivals in the Sufi order of the Tijāniyya, ventured to counter this fatwa by asking the opinion of the ulema of Qayrawān, the famous religious centre in Tunisia. The latter maintained that, having resisted as much as could reasonably be demanded, the Muslim tribes of Algeria might submit to the French without becoming unbelievers, provided that the French neither interfered with their practice of Islam nor violated the honour of their women. Toward the middle of the nineteenth century, three of the four Sunnī schools of jurisprudence adopted this view, even as parts of India seethed with the Wahhābī call to jihād against infidel domination.

As these examples indicate, the issue has to do in part with the history of 'canonical' interpretation and in part also, inevitably, with competition among authorities – the establishment ulema, the Sufi brotherhoods, the jihādist leaders, the rival centres of political power. Judgement is looked for, not only on the Muslims' duty in response to unbelievers, but also on the notion of Muslim faithfulness. One is only a small step from outright condemnation of Muslim leaders for lack of opposition to or, worse, collaboration with non-Islamic powers. Such is the force of one contemporary critique of the governments of the Muslim world, whose leaders are accused of having sold out by, in effect, transforming their societies into forward outposts of the infidel, imperialist West. Some Islamists have gone so far as to conclude that, as a juristic category, *dār al-islām* (the domain of Islam) no longer obtains, given that in no part of the world can an 'Islamic government' be said to exist. (One is bound to note the irony here of Muslims, otherwise victims of a tendency to depict Islam as an indistinct monolith, themselves engaging, in respect of Muslim societies, in huge generalizations that erase all distinctions.) It is no surprise that Ibn Taymiyya – in contrast to what received opinions (the learned and the Islamist) claim – should have understood the dangers of such an approach and, far from being its source, renounced a theology of revolt.

Ibn Taymiyya is not the arch-radical that many today would like him to have been. No more is he, necessarily, the arch-conservative he is made out to be by those political and religious establishments in the Muslim world that approve of him. This might suggest the existence of two Ibn Taymiyyas – one encouraging confrontation and subversive, the other accommodating and submissive to the State. However, as Michot reminds us, while we may read this thinker in many ways, our interpretation must be disciplined by the context in which he operated. And, according to Michot's definitive reading, Ibn Taymiyya affirmed a critical distinction between the external and internal domains. External threat may well demand a militant response for the defence of Islam. But the integrity of the internal domain is conditional on the recognition of the primary importance and authority of the moral framework of order – even if that recognition leads in practice to injustices such as, in his case, incarceration.

The six modern authors, whose readings of Ibn Taymiyya's Mardin fatwa are presented and discussed in this book, commit the sin of (at least) anachronism in giving modern connotations to the words of Ibn Taymiyya or, more precisely, in tying their version of Ibn Taymiyya to modern circumstances. Further, they politicize faith in the name of the Damascene master without realizing the extent to which, in doing so, they violate his ideas. Far from adopting the political route of revolution, Ibn Taymiyya ridiculed the political aspirations of the philosophers. Michot seems to be evoking him when he dismisses the 'Mongolizing' tendency of some (not all) Islamists – namely, the tendency to exploit a politicized version of Islam in order to devalue or invalidate the faith of other Muslims in favour of some greater cause of their own contrivance.

Yahya Michot's career as a scholar has combined, in a rounded whole, painstaking erudition with public engagement. In this explicit commentary on the political legacy of Ibn Taymiyya, he has turned a lifetime of research to great advantage, presenting a learned corrective to the imaginary construction of the Shaykh al-Islām. It is a thesis of immense importance to students of both Islamic thought and modern politics. For an author who has not escaped controversy and criticism, it constitutes a defiant and courageous challenge to all those who arrogate to themselves the right to speak on behalf of the Truth.

James Piscatori
August 2004

Madrasa Qāsimiyya, Mardin (end of 7th/14th c.)
Drawing by PARRY, *Six Months in a Syrian Monastery*, facing p. 153

بسم الله الرحمن الرحيم

Muḥammad is the Messenger of God. Those who are with him are severe towards the unbelievers, compassionate amongst themselves. (Qurʾān, *al-Fatḥ*, 48. 29)

Among the fundamentals of the truth, which the texts [to which one refers to know the religion] provide proofs of, is that people with a tyrannical (*jāʾir*) and unjust (*ẓālim*) leader are ordered to show patience (*ṣabr*) in the face of his tyranny, his injustice, his oppression (*baghī*), and not to fight him. The Prophet, may God pray over him and grant him peace, has likewise commanded that in more than one ḥadīth. He did not, absolutely, authorize the pushing back of oppression by fighting (*qitāl*) [it]. Quite the contrary: given that fighting is the source of dissension (*fitna*), he prohibited the pushing back of oppression by this means and ordered patience. (IBN TAYMIYYA, *al-Istiqāma*, i. 32)

فإن المهاجر من هجر السيئات

Fa-inna l-muhājir man hajara l-sayyiʾāt
'The emigrant (*muhājir*) is one who flees bad deeds'[1]

---

1 Extract from a rough autograph of Ibn Taymiyya, Damascus, Asad National Library 3805, fol. 247^{r}. See below, p. 94.

'Approach to Mardin: City Seated on a Rock'[1]

1 Engraving by Dodd, in J. S. BUCKINGHAM, *Travels*, 177. The engraving by Byfield, reproduced in M. SEVİM, *Anatolia*, ii. 143, does *not*, as the accompanying caption states, depict Mardin, but Bireçik; see J. S. BUCKINGHAM, *Travels*, 26: 'Banks of the Euphrates, and Approach to the Town of Beer'.

Introduction

MARDIN

A crossroads for the major trade routes in the region long known by the name *al-Jazīra* ('the island' – the one formed between the Tigris and Euphrates), the Turkish town of Mardin (*Mārdīn* in Arabic) occupies a strikingly strategic location. It is dominated by a fortress reputed to have been unassailable, from which the view reaches deep into the vast plain of upper Mesopotamia.[1]

At the end of the seventh/thirteenth century, Mardin was the capital of the Artuqid Turkoman statelet of 'the Victorious King' (*al-malik al-manṣūr*), the ageing Najm al-Dīn Ghāzī II (r. 693–712/1294–1312), son of 'the Triumphant King' (*al-malik al-muẓaffar*) Qara Arslān (r. 658–91/1260–92).[2] In point of fact, because his father had not long since

---

1 See V. Minorsky & C. E. Bosworth, *EI*[2] art. 'Mārdīn'; GABRIEL, *Voyages archéologiques dans la Turquie Orientale* (1940), i. 3–44, ii. pl. a–e, I–XXV; BAŞGELEN, *Bir zamanlar Mardin* (2000); MISIRLIOĞLU (ed.), *Mardin: Poetry of Stone and Faith* (1998). ABŪ L-FIDĀʾ (d. 732/1331) speaks of an 'impregnable citadel that none is capable of taking by force' (*Kitāb Taqwīm al-buldān*, 279). DOLAPÖNÜ *Tarihte Mardin: İtr-el-nardin fi tarih Merdin* (1972), and AYDIN *et al.*, *Mardin: Aşiret, Cemaat, Devlet* (2000), are of little interest for our subject.

2 On the Artuqid dynasty, see BOSWORTH, *New Islamic Dynasties*, 194–96 (*Islamic Dynasties* [1967/1980 edn], 119–20). On Mar-

submitted to the Mongol conqueror Hūlāgū, the realm that Najm al-Dīn Ghāzī II ruled over was merely a satellite of the empire of the Īlkhāns of Iran. The Syrian historian Shihāb al-Dīn al-ᶜUmarī (d. 749/1349) refers to the rulers of Mardin as the 'slaves of the [Mongol] sultan'.[1] By contrast, for the celebrated Persian historian and vizier, Rashīd al-Dīn Faḍl Allāh al-Hamadhānī (d. 718/1318), Najm al-Dīn Ghāzī II was an 'intelligent and perfect *pādishāh*, gifted with sagacity (*kiyāsat*) and perspicacity (*firāsat*)'.[2]

Copper *dirham* of Najm al-Dīn Ghāzī II (Mardin, 698/1298)[3]

---

din during their period, see SHUMAYSĀNĪ, *Madīnat Mārdīn min al-fatḥ al-ᶜarabī ilā sanat 921/1515* (1987), 217–58.

1 AL-ᶜUMARĪ, *Kitāb masālik al-abṣār wa-mamālik al-amṣār*, ed. LECH, *Das mongolische Weltreich* (1968), 86. For IBN KATHĪR (d. 774/1373; *al-Bidāya wa-l-nihāya* [1988], xiv. 70), Najm al-Dīn Ghāzī II was 'a decent and venerable old man, of a perfect constitution, corpulent and fat. Whenever he rode a horse, there was always, lest he should suffer exhaustion, a palanquin behind him for him to ride in.'

2 RASHĪD AL-DĪN, *Jāmiᶜ al-tawārīkh* (1994), ii. 1040. According to SHUMAYSĀNĪ (*Madīnat Mārdīn*, 248), 'al-Manṣūr Najm al-Dīn served Mardin with sincerity and followed an Islamic way in the administration of its affairs and its relations.'

3 From *http://mehmeteti.150m.com/artuqids/EWm17.htm.*

Ibn Baṭṭūṭa (703–79?/1304–78?) stayed in Mardin in 727/1327, during the reign of Shams al-Dīn Ṣāliḥ (r. 712–65/1312–64), the son and second successor of Najm al-Dīn Ghāzī II. According to him – and God knows how many cities his travels had enabled him to visit – Mardin is 'a great city at the foot of a hill, one of the most beautiful, striking and substantially-built cities in [the lands of] Islam, and with the finest bazaars.' Like Marco Polo and al-ʿUmarī, he praised the quality of the cloths manufactured in the town.[1]

Another testimony comes from the merchant and poet Ṣafī al-Dīn al-Ḥillī (d. in Baghdād, 750/1349). He was attracted by the prosperity of the principality and found in it a second homeland. He was welcomed to Mardin by Najm al-Dīn Ghāzī II, becoming a familiar figure and dinner guest (*nadīm*) in his court, and retaining the same favour and position under his son, Shams al-Dīn. Ṣafī al-Dīn celebrated at the same time the generosity of his masters and their attachment to the religion. He notably called them 'restorers of the rents of disunity in the religion', and 're-setters of the broken bone of Islam and the Muslims'.[2]

The population of Mardin was made up of Arabs, Kurds, Turkomans and Arameans. In terms of religious affiliation, it was mixed, Muslim and Syriac Christian. A monastery[3] nearby

---

1 IBN BAṬṬŪṬA, *Riḥla*, trans. GIBB, *Travels of Ibn Baṭṭūṭa* (1956), ii. 352–53; AL-ʿUMARĪ, ed. LECH, *Das mongolische Weltreich*, 97; GABRIEL, *Voyages archéologiques*, i. 5.

2 See BOSWORTH, *Mediaeval Islamic Underworld* (1976), i. 134–38, esp. 137.

3 Dayr al-Zaʿfarān; see illustration, below p. 148. On the Christians of Mardin, see DAGHER & TROUPEAU (eds.) *IBN BUṬLĀN*.

was the seat of the Jacobite church. According to Ibn Baṭṭūta, to the credit of its king Shams al-Dīn Ṣāliḥ 'are works of charity, colleges, and hospices for the supply of food. He has a vizier of high distinction, namely, the learned imām [...] Jamāl al-Dīn al-Sinjārī; he studied in the city of Tabrīz and under the great scholars [of the past generation]. His Grand Qāḍī is [...] a man of sound religion, scrupulosity and virtue. He often holds his judicial sessions in the courtyard of a mosque, outside the college, in which he used to perform his devotions.'[1] This important testimony confirms that Mardin's being a part of the Mongol empire of Iran was no hindrance to the activities of its religious authorities, nor to the apparently normal functioning of its Islamic institutions, whether in connection with teaching or charitable works or *fiqh* (jurisprudence) or devotional life.

That said, the proximity of the northern frontier of the Mamlūk sultanate of Cairo, the other great Middle Eastern power of the period and enemy of the Mongols, turned the land into a hazard zone.[2] Caught between the rock and hard

---

Le banquet des prêtres (2004): Ibn Buṭlān (d. 1066) places a parish priest in Mardin at the beginning of the eleventh century.

1 IBN BAṬṬŪṬA, trans. GIBB, *The Travels of Ibn Baṭṭūṭa*, ii. 354.

2 On the political situation in the Near East around 700/1300, some useful information may be found in the Chronology and Map (Appendix, below pp. 149–169, 153). Also, see: IBN TAYMIYYA, *Majmūᶜ al-fatāwā*, trans. MICHOT, 'Textes spirituels XIII' (1995), 26–27; MICHOT, *Lettre à un roi croisé* (1995), 9–27 (map, p. 49); 'Rashīd al-Dīn et Ibn Taymiyya' (2001); AMITAI-PREISS, 'Mongol Imperial Ideology and the Ilkhanid War against the Mamluks' (1999).

place of these two powers, the prince of Mardin could not, to the extent he might have wished, indulge his passion for gardens:[1] instead, he was forced into continual manoeuvring to please first one and then the other.[2] For all that, at the

---

1 See AL-ʿAYNĪ (d. 855/1451), *ʿIqd al-jumān fī taʾrīkh ahl al-zamān. ʿAṣr salāṭīn al-Mamālīk* (1990), iii. 366; GABRIEL, *Voyages archéologiques*, i. 41.

2 Typical in this respect was the way he managed to avoid having to join the Tatar army when, in the spring of 698/1299, the īlkhān Ghāzān (r. 694–703/1295–1304) marched on Sivas accompanied by various Mamlūk emirs who had recently come over to his side, among them Sayf al-Dīn Qibjaq, former deputy-ruler of Damascus.

'The Tatars reached up to Sinjār, Raʾs al-ʿAyn and Mardin. The sovereign of Mardin sent ahead some supplies for them, as well as readying numerous presents and gifts. He also prepared his troops to join company with them but did not go down to [meet] the Tatars, lest Sayf al-Dīn Qibjaq had reported to them about him that he was in correspondence with the Muslims [that is to say, with the Mamlūk sultanate]. He accordingly offered by way of excuse that he was ill, incapable of sitting down and, necessarily therefore, of standing up. They accepted this excuse on account of the gifts and presents with which he had sated their eyes. It is reported that before the Tatars reached his realm, he had strengthened the citadel [of Mardin] with provisions and means sufficient for a period of two years. God was kind to him on this occasion in that they passed by the [town] and did him no harm.' (IBN AL-JAZARĪ, *Taʾrīkh ḥawādith al-zamān* (1998), i. 436; || AL-YŪNĪNĪ, *Dhayl Mirʾāt al-zamān*, trans. GUO, *Early Mamluk Syrian Historiography* (1998), i. 121–22.) Najm al-Dīn Ghāzī II would have less luck with the Syrian emirs who unexpectedly entered Mardin some weeks later.

Notwithstanding the labours of Najm al-Dīn Ghāzī II to preserve a degree of autonomy vis-à-vis his Mongol suzerain,

beginning of Ramaḍān 698/June 1299, the Mardin region was raided by some Syrian emirs.[1] A few months later, these destructive raids would serve as pretext for the īlkhān

---

it is a fact that the Tatars felt at home in Mardin. When, for example, at the beginning of 698/January 1299, Sayf al-Dīn Qibjaq set out east to join up with the īlkhān Ghāzān, he was received in Mardin by both its prince and the Mongol general Būlāhim – or Būlāy (AL-YŪNĪNĪ, trans. GUO, *Early Mamluk Syrian Historiography*, i. 112). Later, Najm al-Dīn Ghāzī II would give his daughter, Dunyā Khātūn, in marriage to Ghāzān's successor, the īlkhān Öljāytū (see IBN BAṬṬŪṬA, trans. GIBB, *Travels of Ibn Baṭṭūṭa*, ii. 353 n. 288; 337, n. 218). The double game that Najm al-Dīn Ghāzī II was playing – as evidenced by his secret correspondence with Damascus and Cairo – was all the more risky. Another example of these contacts: the emir Shams al-Dīn b. al-Taytī, vizier to the prince of Mardin, was named among the delegation which, in the summer of 700/1301, al-Nāṣir Muḥammad the sultan of Cairo wanted to send to the īlkhān Ghāzān (AL-YŪNĪNĪ, trans. GUO, *Early Mamluk Syrian Historiography*, i. 184).

1 See ABŪ L-FIDĀʾ, *al-Mukhtaṣar fī akhbār al-bashar* (n.d.), iv. 42; RASHĪD AL-DĪN, *Jāmiᶜ al-tawārīkh*, ii. 1289–90; the detailed account of AL-ᶜAYNĪ (*ᶜIqd al-jumān*, iii. 365–66), which dates these events to Ramaḍān 696/June 1297 and depicts the aged Najm al-Dīn Ghāzī II as shouting down to the invaders, from the heights of his citadel, not to destroy his favourite garden, *al-Firdaws* (Paradise), to the south-east of the town; SHUMAYSĀNĪ, *Madīnat Mārdīn*, 253–55, which places these raids in 697/1297; AMITAI-PREISS, 'Mongol Imperial Ideology', 66. On that garden (*al-Firdaws*), see TABBAA, 'The Medieval Islamic Garden: Typology and Hydraulics' (1992), 313–14.

Ghāzān Maḥmūd to cross the Euphrates and push toward Damascus.[1]

Silver *dirham* of Ghāzān Maḥmūd (699/1299)[2]

At the beginning of this twenty-first century, Mardin remains one of the most attractive cities in southeast Turkey. However, the majesty of the site, the wealth of its architecture and the importance of its Christian legacy are not the only reasons for its renown: Mardin is in fact regularly alluded to in contemporary Islamic and Islamist writings, at times indeed in the most extreme and violent of them.

The reason for that is that during the period when, under the Muslim dynasty of the Artuqids, Mardin was a small protectorate of the Tatars, it was the subject of a fatwa of Shaykh al-Islām Ibn Taymiyya (d. 728/1328),[3] mainly on the question of its status (in terms of Islamic Law) as 'a domain

---

1 See MICHOT, *Lettre à un roi croisé*, 29; AMITAI-PREISS, 'Mongol Imperial Ideology', 66; AL-YŪNĪNĪ, trans. GUO, *Early Mamluk Syrian Historiography*, i. 182–83, 194–95.

2 From: *http//mehmeteti.150m.com/ilkhanids/UE1817.htm.*

3 On Ibn Taymiyya, see LAOUST, *Essai sur les doctrines*, and 'La biographie d'Ibn Taymīya d'après Ibn Kathīr' (1942–43); also the 'Chronology' in the Appendix, below pp. 149–169.

of peace' or 'a domain of war', with the consequent necessity, or not, of quitting it by *hijra* – emigration to an Islamic land. The fatwa would appear, brief though it is, to have become an inescapable reference for many politico-religious debates among today's Muslims.

Nothing in the text of this Taymiyyan fatwa on Mardin enables it to be dated with any precision to before or during or after the devastating raids into the region by the Mamlūks in Ramaḍān 698/June 1299.[1] To my knowledge,[2] in the whole body of the edited works of the Shaykh al-Islām, there is no other mention elsewhere of Mardin except for the strange tale of a vision of a jinn having borrowed his identity, which is without relevance to the issues of the Legal (*sharᶜī*) status of a territory and the duty of emigration (*hijra*).[3] This means,

---

1 I am not even certain of being able to date the Mardin fatwa to the period directly before or after these raids, roughly the eighteen years of the reign of Najm al-Dīn Ghāzī II.

2 That is, following a search on the word 'Mardin' in the CD-ROMs of Ibn Taymiyya's *Majmūᶜ al fatāwā* and *Muʾallafāt.*

3 'Sometimes [a jinn] approaches someone – it could be a king or a great emir, and an unbeliever – who finds himself alone in the desert, separated from his companions, thirsty, and fearful of death. [The jinn] approaches him in human form, and offers him drink, invites him to become Muslim and leads him to repent. So he converts at his hand. [The jinn] leads him to repent, feeds him, and shows him the way. [The new convert] says to him: "Who are you?", and the [jinn] says to him: "I am So-and-so." He is [for sure] one of the believing jinns.

'A similar thing happened, concerning me, while I was [imprisoned] in Cairo in the citadel.* A similar thing happened [indeed] to a great** Turkish [i.e. Mongol] emir in the region of the East. This person [who introduced himself to the emir]

said to him: "I am Ibn Taymiyya." This emir had no doubt that it was me and informed the king of Mardin of this [happening]. The king of Mardin sent to the king of Cairo a messenger [who informed him] about this story while I was imprisoned [in the citadel]. They made a big deal of it, given the fact that I had not left the prison! But it was a jinn who loved us and who had done with the Turk, the Tatar, something of the same sort as I had done with them when they came to Damascus: I had invited them to become Muslim and, when one of them uttered the two testimonies of faith, I gave them something to eat. [The jinn] thus acted with this [emir]*** just as I had acted. In so doing he wished to honour me so that this [emir] would think that it was I who had done that [to him].

'A group of people said to me: "Why could it not have been an angel?" I said: "No: an angel does not lie. For this one said: 'I am Ibn Taymiyya' knowing that in so saying he was lying."'
(IBN TAYMIYYA, *Majmūᶜ al-fatāwā*, xiii. 92–93)

* Ibn Taymiyya was imprisoned in the citadel of Cairo from 26 Ramaḍān 705/11 April 1306 to 25 Rabī I 707/23 September 1307. See 'Chronology', Appendix, below pp. 156–161.
** kabīr : kathīr **F**. ***maᶜa-hu : maᶜa-hum **F**.

It is proper to note a small collection of fatwas (see IBN TAYMIYYA, *al-Masāʾil al-mārdīniyya* [1980]) that comprises responses to questions coming from Mardin. This collection relates to specific points of Islamic Law – cleanliness and purity, the prayer rite, fasting, ablutions, commercial transactions, alms-tax, marriage, Legal penalties, charitable endowments *(waqf)*, debts – without relevance to the content of the fatwa studied here. Ibn Taymiyya does not allude therein to Mardin, even when called upon to deal with commercial relations with the Tatars (*ibid.*, 141–43; also, see below, p. 64, n. 1). IBN ᶜABD AL-HĀDĪ (d. 744/1343) mentions in his bibliography of Ibn Taymiyya (*al-ᶜUqūd al-durriyya min manāqib [Ibn] Taymiyya*, 56) a *Response to a Question Coming from Mardin.*

significantly, that there is no mention at all of Mardin in the three famous anti-Mongol fatwas of Ibn Taymiyya – the other obligatory references for contemporary Islamist extremism.[1] As for the historians of the Mamlūk period, they provide no fact enabling a better acquaintance with the circumstances in which the Mardin fatwa was issued.

That being the case, is there really no other resource that can enrich our understanding of the Mardin fatwa? Far from it. Without going so far as to risk according to the thought of the Shaykh al-Islām an over-systematic quality, it is indeed possible to correlate this writing with other pieces by Ibn Taymiyya on the *hijra*, as well as on the concepts of *dār al-islām* ('domain of Islam'), *dār al-kufr* ('domain of unbelief'), etc. It is the approach favoured here[2] – whence the translation, following the fatwa of Mardin, of three other texts by the Shaykh al-Islām, which in turn will be clarified by reference, in the notes, to several other extracts from his works.

---

1 See the passages translated in MICHOT, 'Textes spirituels XI–XIII' (1994–95).

2 For this intertextual approach, it is impossible, in the present state of study of the corpus of Ibn Taymiyya's works, to offer a chronological perspective.

AN ETHIC OF BALANCE

Ibn Taymiyya's judgement is that a Muslim in Mardin 'disabled from putting his religion into effect (*iqāma*)'[1] must emigrate to the lands of Islam. In the opposite case, that is if he is able to practise, that 'remains preferable but is not obligatory'. It is not difficult to imagine the sort of question that, at the time, his interlocutor would be keen to address to Ibn Taymiyya: how could there any longer be a duty to emigrate, to leave in *hijra*, when the Prophet said: 'No more *hijra* after the conquest [of Makka]…'?

The question is a classic one, and numerous of the learned scholars of classical Islam, before and after Ibn Taymiyya, have put forward various answers to it.[2] As for the tenor of Ibn Taymiyya's own thinking on the matter, there are, happily, other texts of his available to define it.

Text II below, translated under the heading 'The true emigrant (*muhājir*)', is taken from Ibn Taymiyya's commentary on the famous ḥadīth on intention: 'Deeds are valued only according to the intentions and each man has to his

---

1 Quotations given without references in this Introduction (as here) come from texts that are translated in the main body of this work, where they can be easily found and followed up.

2 See MASUD, 'The Obligation to Migrate: the Doctrine of *Hijra* in Islamic Law' (1990), 33–42; BASHIER, *Hijra: Story and Significance* (1983), 89–91; MADELUNG, 'Has the Hijra come to an end?' (1986). Montgomery Watt's article 'Hid̲j̲ra' in EI^2 has no bearing on the question here.

account only that which he intended. The one whose *hijra* is made to God and His Messenger, his *hijra* is made to God and His Messenger. The one whose *hijra* is made to a this-worldly end that he attains or to a woman that he marries, his *hijra* is made to that to which he emigrated.'[1] This tradition provided the Damascene theologian the opportunity to explore the concepts of *hijra* and *muhājir* (emigrant).

According to him the full meaning that certain words connote is to be sought beyond their apparent sense. Thus the Messenger also said: 'The *muhājir* is one who flees that which God has forbidden.' In short, the true emigrant is not one who quits his land, but one who flees sin. Various other Prophetic sayings, notably on the qualities – 'warrior', 'Muslim', 'believer', 'poor', 'ruined', 'childless', 'strong' – invite one to look beyond the immediate sense of the words and seek out the deeper reality of these qualities. The 'strong', for example, is not the one who, being enraged, wrestles you down, but only he who, in the event of anger, remains in possession of himself.

That understood, no difficulty remains in continuing to speak of *hijra* even after the Prophet's saying 'No more *hijra* after the conquest [of Makka]…'

The first of two complementary strands of argument for doing so is that the *hijra* the Prophet had in mind in speaking thus was the one 'to which people were used in his time,

---

1 See in particular AL-BUKHĀRĪ, *Ṣaḥīḥ*, *Badʾ al-waḥy*, i. 6 (*ʿĀlam.* 1); MUSLIM, *Ṣaḥīḥ*, *Imāra*, vi. 48 (*ʿĀlam.* 3530); IBN ḤANBAL, *Musnad*, i. 25 (*ʿĀlam.* 163). For Ibn Taymiyya's commentary, see *Majmūʿ al-fatāwā*, xviii. 244–85.

namely the *hijra* towards Madina, departing from Makka or some other [regions] of the land of the Arabs'. To emigrate was then a Legal obligation since Madina was the domain of Islam and of the faith, Makka and the rest of Arabia being the domain of unbelief and war. When, after that, 'Makka was conquered and became a domain of Islam, with the Arabs entering into Islam, this land [of Arabia] as a whole became a domain of Islam'. It was then no longer justifiable to emigrate to Madina; nor, conversely, was it justifiable for the Makkan Companions (who had not long since emigrated to Madina) to return to Makka. In the historical sense of the term, to do the *hijra* is thus an injunction that has lost its rationale and, in consequence, is no longer one.[1] From which point Ibn Taymiyya goes on to stress, logically enough, the continuation of the ḥadīth 'No more *hijra* after the conquest…': '…but jihād and good intention [remain]! And when you are called [to jihād], go to it!'

The second strand of argument is that to be an emigrant (*muhājir*) in the true sense of the term as defined by the Prophet – that is, as 'one who flees that which God has prohibited' – will remain a duty always, in all times and all places. Thus the Prophet stated: 'The *hijra* shall by no means be suspended so long as the enemy remains to be fought.' Ibn Taymiyya says explicitly that this ḥadīth is every bit as true as the ḥadīth 'No more *hijra* after the conquest…'

---

1 On this point, see MADELUNG, 'Has the Hijra come to an end?', according to whom the duty of *hijra*, this time to Syria, was re-introduced by caliph ʿUmar and the Umayyads. See also BASHIER, *Hijra: Story and Significance*, 90.

Quoting the Qurʾānic verse (*al-Naḥl*, 16. 110) – 'As for those who emigrated (*hājara*) after they had been tested, then fought and were steadfast, assuredly your Lord, after such things, is indeed forgiving, merciful' – the Shaykh al-Islām further observes: 'What is signified by these [words] concerns every individual whom Satan has tested [in order to distance him] from his religion or whom he causes to fall into disobedience, who then flees from (*hajara*) evil deeds, fights against himself and other enemies, fights against the hypocrites by bidding to the good and forbidding from the reprehensible, etc., and who is patient and persevering in the face of whatever strikes him – [of] word or deed.' In the fully rounded sense of the term, doing *hijra* thus begins in fleeing one's own sin, fighting against oneself, repentance (*tawba*). As for departing in *hijra* to some other place, geographically speaking, that is to be understood as a particular manifestation of this movement toward interior reform. 'For a man to emigrate (*hijra*),' Ibn Taymiyya writes, 'from a place of unbelief and disobedience to a place of faith and obedience is like his repenting and passing from unbelief and disobedience to faith and obedience: it is a command that will remain [in force] until the Day of Resurrection.'

Text III, *A Double Reality*, was perhaps written in response to a question that has not been preserved. It should serve to complement Ibn Taymiyya's commentary on the Qurʾānic verse *al-Naḥl*, 16. 110, at the close of Text II. Indeed, the theologian explains therein, on the basis of verses of the Qurʾān and various events from the early period of Islam, that: 'turning away (*hijra*) from perverts is [a reality] of two kinds: turning away as [sheer] quitting (*hijra tark*) and turning away in order to inflict a penalty (*hijra taʿzīr*).' The first kind of fleeing aims to achieve distance and separation from evil actions and from those servants of evil whose company is harmful. 'The emigration (*hijra*) of a Muslim quitting the domain of war (*dār al-ḥarb*)' constitutes one particular instance of that. As for the second kind of fleeing, it constitutes a form of punishment for whoever is the object of it, and is connected to the general duty of bidding to the good and forbidding from the reprehensible. It is important to note that Ibn Taymiyya is at pains to mention the necessity of weighing the pros and cons of either sort of *hijra*, whose outcomes must never be worse than the evil or wrong, for action against which they were envisaged and ventured.

In Text IV *Appropriate Severity*, Ibn Taymiyya analyses the reasons for and the meaning of the prudent reserve formerly observed by Aḥmad b. Ḥanbal (d. 241/855) with regard to the partisans of the Muʿtazilī heresy of the Qurʾān's being created.[1] As in Text III and in an analogous manner he is led to speak on this subject of a double reality to the meaning of *hijra*. At one point he distinguishes the act of fleeing sin and sinners for fear of God (*hijrat al-taqwā*) as a form of abandoning and renouncing that amounts to addressing to them a 'reminder'. At another, he speaks of the act of fleeing as a penalty (*hijra taʿzīr*) and chastisement of the transgressors

---

1 The doctrine of the Qurʾān's being created was enforced by the ʿAbbāsid caliph al-Maʾmūn and his successors between 213/833 and 234/848. Ibn Ḥanbal played an important role in rejection and eventual defeat of this State-imposed rationalist theology. See M. Hinds, *EI*[2] art. 'Miḥna'.

and the unjust which constitutes a form of jihād, is connected with the general duty of bidding to the good and forbidding from the reprehensible, and relates to the implementation of the Legal sanctions (*ḥadd*).

Nevertheless, the Shaykh al-Islam insists once again, and more forcefully than in Text III, on the conditions to be met before undertaking either type of *hijra.* The powers in play on the side of the good and the evil must be compared. The gain that accrues to the religion from taking action as envisaged, or from not taking action, must be balanced, as also their consequences and their potential secondary outcomes. Thus, forethought and pragmatism become necessary. Turning away/punishing is not always useful nor, it therefore follows, is it obligatory. The way that Ibn Ḥanbal advised for coping with the Jahmīs,[1] given the power they disposed at the time, testifies to that approach; so too the fact that the early scholars continued to accept the ḥadīths transmitted by Baṣrans despite the latter being advocates of the doctrine of free will. At times there is a price to be paid for 'implementing the obligations related to [obtaining] knowledge, to [waging] jihād, etc.', and if paying that price is less serious than would be leaving the obligation in question, one must opt for the lesser evil.

---

1 The disciples of Jahm b. Ṣafwān, Abū Muḥriz (d. 128/746), partisans of the doctrine of stripping bare the divine essence and the rejection of His attributes. See IBN TAYMIYYA, *Majmūᶜ al-fatāwā*, trans. MICHOT, 'Textes spirituels VIII' (1992–93), 15; 'XV' (1996), 26–27; W. M. Watt, *EI²* art. 'D̲jahm b. Ṣafwān', 'D̲jahmiyya'.

In truth, every case is a unique case. Ibn Taymiyya insists accordingly upon the necessary circumspection and cautions against generalization. The counsels of Ibn Ḥanbal and other early imāms were bound to context and occasion. The dicta of the Prophet, bearing upon concrete particulars, are valid only for similar cases. Those who, from such counsels or dicta, make up general, universal rulings supposedly self-applying, automatic, mechanical – notably on the question of *hijra*, rejection, ostracism, punishment – fall into an extremism as grave as the extremism of those who turn away from all forms of fleeing sin, and of bidding to the good and forbidding from the reprehensible. The religion, as the theologian reminds us once more, is a just balance. In practice, it becomes a middle way between zero-tolerance and absolute leaving-be.

When the four distinct texts presented below are considered together, they testify to the complexity of Ibn Taymiyya's understanding and treatment of the theme of *hijra*. Indeed, its complexity is such that it becomes difficult to translate the word in a uniform way. After the historical *Hijra* of the Prophet and his Companions during the formative period of Islam, *hijra* (in the most ordinary sense of the term, or inwardly, as the quitting of sin, turning away from or prosecuting the agents of evil) has a reality astonishing for its plurality. That said, three clear conclusions will claim our attention.

'Must I emigrate to a domain of Islam?' is a question that a number of Muslims living in the West, or in countries that seem to them to undermine those countries' formal Islamic identity, continue to ask themselves.[1] At times the question leads to dramatic consequences when a response in the affirmative has been accompanied by a general anathematization of others and self-marginalization, by escapist retreat into an imaginary world of the Pure, or resort to violence in diverse forms, sometimes extreme …[2] For Ibn Taymiyya, the answer to be given to such a question is anything but automatic and predetermined, and depends fundamentally on the capacity to give practical effect to the religion (*iqāmat al-dīn*). To be sure, the concept is not very precise and may entail much more than the simple practice of Islam as – might one say – a conscientious expression of 'civic and familial responsibility'. However, what is beyond doubt is that, in the fatwa of Mardin, Ibn Taymiyya speaks of it in the singular, not the plural. Then, this giving practical effect to the religion, is in the first instance, an individual personal matter, not collective, not communitarian – the more so, following the Messenger's explanation that 'the emigrant (*muhājir*) is the one who flees that which God has prohibited'. And it is in sound relationship to this Prophetic teach-

---

1 See for example, on the internet, the question 'Is the *hijra* still obligatory?' addressed in May 2003 to the fatwa service at: *www.islam-online.net/fatwa/english/FatwaDisplay.asp?hFatwaID=99040*.

2 See the example of the Egyptian group of Shukrī Muṣṭafā (d. 1977) *al-Takfīr wa-l-hijra* (Excommunication and Emigration); KEPEL, *Le Prophète et Pharaon. Aux sources des mouvements islamistes* (1993), 73–108; also: I. Yusuf, *OEMIW* art. 'Hijrah'; and WEBSTER, 'Hijra and the Dissemination of Wahhābī Doctrine in Saudi Arabia' (1993).

ing on the true meaning of *hijra* that, according to the Shaykh al-Islām, the question must be approached. That means also, bearing in mind the more or less sinful nature of our own interior domain, a due circumspection when we pronounce judgement on others, and – whether it is a matter of simply holding ourselves aloof from sin and sinners or of combating them – a prudent weighing up of the outcomes that our actions will have for the religion.

The second conclusion, in direct extension of the first: Ibn Taymiyya's thinking on the *hijra*, as exemplified in the four texts discussed here, is essentially of an ethical nature and is typically elaborated in terms of the religion – it is not, in the narrow sense of that term, political. The theologian interests himself in the conditions of the souls much more than in society, in God's Law (*sharīʿa*) and the fight against sin much more than in the laws of the city and its organization. The very terms he uses authenticate that concern: there is no question, for instance, of 'Islamic government' (*al-ḥukm bi-l-islām*)[1] or of an 'Islamic regime' (*niẓām*). The Damascene shaykh does speak, it is true, towards the end of the Mardin fatwa, of the 'Islamic institutions' (*aḥkām al-islām*),[2] but the term for him relates more closely to Islamic

---

1 If one may judge from a CD-ROM search of *Muʾallafāt*, the phrase 'Islamic government' (*al-ḥukm bi-l-islām*) is absent from the entire corpus of the digitalized works of Ibn Taymiyya.

2 'Whoever outwardly (*ẓāhir*) accepts Islam, the external institutions of Islam (*aḥkām al-islām al-ẓāhira*) must act for him: the protection of his person and his property for example, marriage, inheritance, and the like things. To this end, the simple outward confession [of faith] suffices, even if one does not

jurisprudence (*fiqh*) than to a political system, and in the case here, he does not use it directly with regard to emigration.

Third conclusion: the profound utilitarianism of Ibn Taymiyya in the matter of practical morality and religion is strikingly confirmed by the prudence, the spirit of reserve and the pragmatism that he shows in these texts on the subject of the two forms of *hijra*, of bidding to the good and forbidding from the reprehensible, and of jihād. This utilitarianism will no doubt surprise an uninformed reader. His disavowal of ill-considered and risky ventures, as also his critique of extremism in intolerance or in indulgence, should serve to polish the image of a theologian of moderation, an image very different from the one often presented of him nowadays.

The Taymiyyan concept of *hijra* clarified in this way, it remains to ask what exactly the Shaykh al-Islām understood by the phrases 'domain of peace' and 'domain of war' that he

---

know what there is within [the heart of] the man [in question].' (IBN TAYMIYYA, *Darʾ taʿāruḍ al-ʿaql wa-l-naql* (1979), vii. 434)

'Whoever is, outwardly, a Muslim, the external institutions of Islam must act for him, be it in the matter of marriage, inheritance, washing [his corpse], praying over [it], and burial in the cemetery of the Muslims, etc.' (IBN TAYMIYYA, *Majmūʿ al-fatāwā*, xxiv. 285)

At the beginning of his principal anti-Mongol fatwa, Ibn Taymiyya exemplifies the act of instituting 'according to what the Book and the Tradition [*Sunna*] institute' by mentioning 'life, property, reputation, marriage contracts, etc.' (*Majmūʿ al-fatāwā*, xxviii. 510; trans. MICHOT, 'Textes spirituels XI', 29).

uses at the end of the Mardin fatwa.[1] Here again, an intertextual clarification is fortunately possible, deriving in this case mainly from Text II and certain other pieces translated in the accompanying notes. Ibn Taymiyya's reflection on the *Hijra* of the Prophet from Makka to Madina leads him in fact to wonder about the status of the two towns at this time. For Ibn Taymiyya, the answer leaves no room for doubt: though it was in itself 'the Mother of cities' and 'the land most beloved of God and His Messenger', Makka was still 'a domain of unbelief and war' (*dār kufr wa ḥarb*) whereas 'faith was in Madina', in exile. But 'when Makka was conquered and became a domain of Islam, with the Arabs entering into Islam, this land [of Arabia] as a whole became a domain of Islam'.

That is to say, the status of domain of war or of peace, of unbelief or of Islam, of perversity or of faith, etc., is not an essential intrinsic quality that of necessity goes with an entity, in this case a city or region, or that flows necessarily from some 'nature' that it possesses, or what, in short, the theologian calls (in fine Avicennan style) a necessary concomitant

---

1 On these concepts, see: A. Abel, *EI²* art. 'Dār al-ḥarb', 'Dār al-islām'; M.-R. Djalili, *OEMIW* art. 'Dār al-ḥarb'; R. Peters, *OEMIW* art. 'Dār al-islām'; RAMADAN, *Être Musulman Européen*, 202–46 (1999; re-used in his *Dār ash-shahāda: l'Occident, espace du témoignage* (2002), 21–76, and *Musulmans de l'Occident et l'avenir de l'islam* (2003), 113–38); BASHIER, *Hijra: Story and Significance*, 90–94; among the many internet accessible fatwas, SAQR, *Concept of Dar al-Islam and Dar al-Harb* (2002); MAWLAWI, *Dar al-Kufr: An Abode of Daʿwah, not War* (2002).

(*lāzim*). It is at most 'an accidental [attribute], correlative to the [city or region's] inhabitants'.

The various texts in which Ibn Taymiyya comes back to this topic are unanimous: the status of a city or region is defined as a function of its inhabitants, according to whether they are believers, Muslims, virtuous, or the opposite. And this status changes and is altered as their 'situation', that is, the condition of their souls, changes. The comparisons he offers could not be more telling. When a mosque becomes a tavern, a place of perversity or a church, and vice versa, 'its [status] is correlative to [the condition of] its occupants'. When a virtuous man becomes a perverted one, a believer an unbeliever, and vice versa, '[the status] of each is correlative to the transition of [his] conditions (*ḥāl*) from one condition to another.'

The opportunity to stress the primary importance accorded in Islam to action, to the *praxis mystica*, is too good for our theologian to miss and, with the voluntarism for which he is well known, he seizes it, with reminder, naturally, of the superiority of standing guard (*ribāṭ*) in the strongholds on the frontiers (*thaghr*) over settling in Makka, Madina or Jerusalem.[1] Whatever the eminent qualities of the three towns, 'the best land, for what is of merit for any man, is a land where he is more obedient to God and His Messenger'.

The subject demands an extensive study in its own right but would take us too far from our purpose here. The

---

1 On the virtues of Jerusalem according to Ibn Taymiyya, see MATTHEWS, 'A Muslim Iconoclast (Ibn Taymiyyeh) on the "Merits" of Jerusalem and Palestine' (1936).

meaning that Ibn Taymiyya gives to phrases like 'domain of peace' or 'domain of war' is now clear. He approaches these concepts in a way that is at once both personalist and religious, or ethical. As for politics in the narrow sense of the term, there is no more question of it here than in Ibn Taymiyya's thinking on the *hijra*.

If we now go back to the end of the Mardin fatwa, we can confirm that this was indeed Ibn Taymiyya's perspective, when he affirms for the Mesopotamian city a status that is 'composite'. He refuses to see in it a domain of war because a domain of war, as he writes, is one 'whose inhabitants are unbelievers', which, in the actual instance, is not the case, despite the multi-confessional character of the Mardinan population. What to make, though, of his refusal to see in Mardin a 'domain of peace in which the institutions (*aḥkām*) of Islam are implemented because its army (*jund*) is [composed of] Muslims'? Can the theologian have shifted here to a political approach?

I do not think so. The juridical–religious (rather more than political) character of the phrase 'institutions (*aḥkām*) of Islam' in Ibn Taymiyya's understanding of it was indicated earlier. Besides, it is surely worthwhile fully to grasp the linkage that the theologian establishes between these institutions being in effect and the presence of an army of Muslims, while not saying a word about *civil* authorities. Does not such a forward positioning of the military exclude a priori the very possibility of politics in the noblest sense of the term, and of the State? We will come back to this question later. Taking it up at this stage is, for the purpose of understanding Ibn Taymiyya's refusal to accord the status of domain of peace to Mardin, not essential.

'Standing guard (*murābaṭa*) on the path of God is better than settling (*mujāwara*) in Makka, Madina and Jerusalem'[1]

One may indeed affirm that, according to the Shaykh al-Islām, in order to have a domain of unbelief and war, it is not enough that the institutions in effect there are not Muslim if the population is: the inhabitants must themselves be unbelievers, as is explicitly stated at the end of the Mardin fatwa. Conversely, in order to have a domain of Islam and of peace, it is not enough that the inhabitants are Muslims: there must also be Muslim institutions. In other words, there must be true Muslims, that is, Muslims who put Muslim institutions into effect. In Text II Ibn Taymiyya quotes the ḥadīths defining the true Muslims and the true believers as,

---

1 Two Warriors. Ink drawing on paper, Egypt, fifth/eleventh century. For the quotation, see p. 79, n. 3.

respectively, those 'from whose tongue and hand the Muslims are safe (*salima*)' and 'before whom the people feel themselves to be in security (*amina*), whether in respect of their blood or their possessions'. Further, when he gives examples of what he understands by Muslim institutions it is notably the protection of the Muslims' lives and possessions that he calls to mind[1] – in short, security of person and property.

Being a domain of Islam and of peace constitutes for Ibn Taymiyya, then, an ideal yet to be attained. Alike in the Mardin fatwa as in other texts, he considers that the realization of this ideal is fundamentally to do with individual persons, according to whether they are themselves true Muslims or not, putting the religion into effect or not, in respect of the lives and possessions of the Muslims. In the case of Mardin, about which he cannot have lacked for information – and here it is not a question of a spectator's knowledge, like that of Ibn Baṭṭūṭa – it was the part played by the Tatars in the defence of this Muslim protectorate of the Īlkhāns and the war crimes for which they were all too notorious[2] that most likely prevented the theologian from judging that such an ideal (such a domain of peace for the Muslims there) had

---

1 See above, p. 19 n. 2.

2 See, for example, what Ibn Taymiyya reports of the atrocities committed by the Mongols at the time of their occupation of Damascus in 699/1299–1300, in *Majmūᶜ al-fatāwā*, trans. MICHOT, 'Textes spirituels XI', 30–31. See also: MICHOT, *Lettre à un roi croisé*, 41–46. At the beginning of 716/1316, a band of Tatars attacked, in the market of Mardin, a caravan bound for Syria. The fighting spread to the whole city and wounded numerous of its inhabitants: see SHUMAYSĀNĪ, *Madīnat Mardin*, 256–57.

indeed been attained. In adopting this position, Ibn Taymiyya is far less concerned with the nature of the Artuqid regime in Mardin than with the dangers that weighed on the population of a vassal statelet in the empire of those foreign enemies whom he knew well, and the seriousness of whose recent conversion to Islam he had some doubts about.[1] The thinking of Ibn Taymiyya is of an essentially juridical–religious nature, and personalist. To that is added a concern that is in truth far less political than it is security-oriented, even humanitarian.

Any wolf eager to pounce on Mardin will certainly have been disappointed by Ibn Taymiyya's fatwa. Indeed, whether Mardin is or is not a domain of peace matters little in the end since, in any event – and this is fundamental – the Damascene shaykh refuses to accord to it the status of domain of war, the inhabitants of which would have to be unbelievers.[2] His fatwa is thus quite the opposite of a green light to the unleashing of general hostilities. Rather than see this as sitting on the fence, we will prefer to hold to its measured

---

1 See the anti-Mongol passages of *Majmūᶜ al-fatāwā*, trans. MICHOT, 'Textes spirituels XI–XIII'.

2 For a comparison of the stance of Ibn Taymiyya with the positions taken in classical *fiqh*, see M.-R. DJALILI (*OEMIW*, i. 337): 'From the moment that the leaders of the *dār al-ḥarb* accept Islam, this territory is considered as fully part of *dār al-Islām*. Conversely, an Islamic territory taken by infidels becomes *dār al-ḥarb* when the law of the non-Muslims replaces Islamic Law.' See also: A. Abel, *EI*[2] art. 'Dār al-ḥarb'; R. Peters, *OEMIW* art. 'Dār al-Islām'.

deliberation alongside a deeply religious emphasis on understanding things as a function of persons, not systems. This is already manifest right at the very start of the fatwa, which he opens with a reminder that the lives and possessions of Muslims are forbidden 'wherever they may be, in Mardin or anywhere else'. The more is this so when, in his conclusion, he no longer speaks of Mardin as such, but of its diverse inhabitants, for whom he invites their being treated in light of their merits, according to whether they are Muslims or absconders from the Law of Islam.

SIX MODERN READINGS

The non-existence of definite information about the historical context of the Mardin fatwa has not deterred diverse contemporary authors from making copious use of it in their politico-religious analyses. I translate below six such texts found on the internet by a simple Google-search on the Arabic word *Mārdīn.* Plainly, an inquiry conducted in this way cannot pretend to offer more than a sampling of opinions, and many other modern texts invoking Ibn Taymiyya's fatwa on Mardin might well have been incorporated in it. Be that as it may, the selection offered will nevertheless suffice to give a clear idea of the kind of use to which the thought of the Damascene shaykh has sometimes been subjected by those who, in the present time, appeal to his authority.

Text A, first published in December 1981, is the oldest. It is taken from one of the founding texts of violent Islamism of the end of the twentieth century: *al-Farīḍat al-ghā'iba* ('The Duty Neglected', i.e. left out of our concerns) by the

Egyptian electrician, Muḥammad ʿAbd al-Salām Faraj (1954–82). Likening the contemporary rulers of Muslim countries to the medieval Mongol invaders attacked in various fatwas of Ibn Taymiyya, Faraj inspired the assassins of President Anwar Sadat (d. 6 October 1981), with whom he was executed on 15 April 1982. The Mardin fatwa comes up more than once in his text.[1]

Shaykh ʿAbd Allāh Yūsuf ʿAzzām (1941–89),[2] graduate of al-Azhar, and a member of the Muslim Brotherhood, was one of the first Palestinians to join the anti-Soviet jihād in Afghanistan. He played a dominant role in organizing the 'Islamic Legion' and providing the spiritual support for the Mujāhidīn in battle. He was at one time the teacher, then the mentor and companion, of Usāma b. Lādin. His memory is revered in several Islamist movements, of which *Ḥamās* is one. Frequently citing Ibn Taymiyya, ʿAbd Allāh ʿAzzām

---

1 On *al-Farīḍat al-ghāʾiba*, see JANSEN, *The Neglected Duty* (1986), which contains a translation and analysis of the text, and a discussion of the reactions and refutations it provoked in Egypt; SIVAN, 'Ibn Taymiyya: Father of the Islamic Revolution', 41, 48–50; *Radical Islam, Medieval Theology and Modern Politics* (1990), 103, 127–29; KEPEL, *Le Prophète et Pharaon*, 209–21; *Intellectuels et militants de l'islam contemporain* (1990), 20–22; *Jihad. Expansion et déclin de l'islamisme* (2000), 82–83. The refutation of Faraj in 1402/1982 by the Shaykh al-Azhar JĀD AL-ḤAQQ (*Kutayb al-farīḍat al-ghāʾiba wa-l-radd ʿalay-hi*) is a very interesting 'official' text but does not mention Mardin.

2 See KEPEL, *Jihad*, 144–47, 227–28; SFEIR *& al.*, *Dictionnaire mondial de l'islamisme,* 103–05; BENJAMIN & SIMON, *The Age of Sacred Terror* (2002), 99–100, 103–04; the biographical notes and translated texts at *www.assabyle.com.*

considered jihād an individual obligation, and not just in Afghanistan, but to re-take any land that had once been Muslim – Andalusia, for example. Text B is an extract from his *Iʿlān al-jihād* ('Declaration of Jihād').[1] He draws upon the Mardin fatwa in order to understand the status of Afghanistan under Russian occupation.

The Saudi dissident, Muḥammad b. ʿAbd Allāh al-Masʿarī,[2] son of an important religious personage, and trained as a physicist in the US, was imprisoned for six months in 1993 when the Riyadh government turned on the Islamist opposition represented by the Committee for the Defence of Legitimate Rights (CDLR, founded 1993).[3] Then, in 1994 he settled in England, where he acquired political refugee status. Much in evidence in the media and on the internet, he re-formed the CDLR in London as an ambivalent mix of 'human rights' and Islamism. In 1995 he published *al-Adillat al-qaṭʿiyya ʿalā ʿadam sharʿiyyat al-dawlat al-Saʿūdiyya* ('The Definitive Proofs of the [Religious] Illegitimacy of the Saudi State'), still available on line at the web-site of the Islamic Information Centre

---

1 See *www.geocities.com/ebadteam/images/al-gehad/e3lanalgehad.htm*; ZEIDAN, 'The Islamic Fundamentalist View of Life as a Perennial Battle' (2001), 43–44.

2 See KEPEL, *Jihad*, 221–22; FANDY, *Saudi Arabia and the Politics of Dissent* (1999), 115–47; TEITELBAUM, *Holier than Thou. Saudi Arabia's Islamic Opposition* (2000), 50–66; BUNT, *Virtually Islamic: Computer-mediated Communication and Cyber Islamic Environments* (2000), 92–93.

3 See SFEIR *&* *al.*, *Dictionnaire mondial de l'islamisme*, 75–78; FANDY, *Saudi Arabia and Dissent*, 115–47; TEITELBAUM, *Holier Than Thou*, 49–71.

al-Haramain.[1] The work comprises eleven chapters and four appendices. Text C is taken from the first section of Chapter 11: 'The domain of unbelief and the domain of Islam'. The Mardin fatwa enters the reflections of al-Masʿarī as he develops his argument on the meaning of the two statuses.

Shaykh ʿAbd al-ʿAzīz b. Ṣāliḥ b. Sulaymān al-Jarbūʿ (b. 1387/1967),[2] a graduate of the Sharīʿa faculty of the Imām University in Riyadh, and a Friday preacher in one of that city's renowned mosques, was sentenced to three years in prison when the Saudi authorities brought their Islamist opposition forcefully into line in 1994. A supporter of al-Qāʿida, he has distributed via the internet a detailed analysis seeking to justify the attacks on America of the 11th September 2001, and an apologia for Usāma b. Lādin.[3] He is in addition the author of several works on Islamic jurisprudence (*fiqh*), among them *Kitāb al-Iʿlām bi-wujūb al-hijra min dār al-kufr ilā dār al-islām* ('The Book Informing of the Obligation to Emigrate from the Domain of Unbelief to the Domain of

---

1 *www.alhramain.com/text/kotob/5/f.htm.* See FANDY, *Saudi Arabia and Dissent*, 135–37.

2 See al-Jarbūʿ's internet site *www.geocities.com/aljarbo/alrsail.htm*; JACQUARD, *Au nom d'Oussama Ben Laden…Dossier secret* (2001), 252–57.

3 See HALEVI, 'al-Qaeda's Intellectual Legacy: New Radical Islamic Thinking' (2003); PAZ, '*Qaedat al-jihad*: New Name on the Road to Palestine' (2002); JACQUARD, *Au nom d'Oussama Ben Laden.* The writings of Shaykh al-Jarbūʿ can be read on his internet site or at *www.tawhed.ws/a?i=11*. As Usāma b. Lādin refers regularly to Ibn Taymiyya, I hoped to have been able to find some mention of Mardin among his writings. However, the search has been in vain.

Islam'), completed in Rabīᶜ II 1422/July 2001. Text D is extracted from section 5 of this book: 'The four situations of the emigrant, and their statuses'.[1] For a Muslim incapable of openly practising his religion, he rules that it is obligatory to emigrate from contemporary Arab countries, just as Ibn Taymiyya made obligatory or strongly commended the same in the case of Mardin. Shaykh al-Jarbūᶜ was re-arrested by the Saudi police in 2003.

The last two of the modern texts that will be discussed come from authors less radical than the others. The Syrian Zuhayr Sālim is the director of The Arab Orient Center for Strategic and Civilization Studies in London. Among other of his writings published on his internet site one can read *Waqfāt fī fiqh al-jihād* ('Positions on the law of jihād').[2] Text E is taken from the last of its seven sections. The author there refers to the Mardin fatwa when he questions the division of the world into domain of Islam, domain of war, etc.

Shaykh Saᶜd al-Dīn b. Muḥammad al-Kibbī is director of the Imām al-Bukhārī Institute of Islamic Law in Beirut. He speaks of the Mardin fatwa in a piece entitled *Tabṣīr al-ᶜibād bi-taḥqīq baᶜḍ masāʾil al-jihād* ('Whereby One Makes the Servants [of God] See, by Discovering the Truth about Certain Questions on the Jihād'), which is available on line at the website of the Imām al-Bukhārī Institute.[3] Text F is a

---

1 See *www.khayma.com/wahbi/Research/Now/elam/main.htm.* The text may also be read on Shaykh al-Jarbūᶜ's internet site, or at *www.tawhed.ws/a?i=11.*

2 See *www.asharqalarabi.org.uk/center1/dirasatjehad.htm.*

3 See *www.assiraj.bizland.com/library/jihad.htm.*

brief passage from this study. Shaykh al-Kibbī mentions the Mardin fatwa when he is wondering about the bounds to the duty of jihād.

However interesting it may be to analyse the contents of each of these six texts in themselves, that is not the aim of the discussion that follows. Rather, we shall confine discussion to their bearing on the two major themes drawn from the Mardin fatwa: *hijra* and the statuses of domain of Islam and domain of war.

The first observation justified by a comparison of these six contemporary texts is that their authors – when they do not evince a complete absence of concern for the actual, historical context of the Mardin fatwa – share the same cavalier disregard for medieval history.

Al-Masᶜarī simplifies the historical reality by writing: 'the land of Mardin […] had fallen under the rule of the unbelieving Tatars.' Sālim gets it even more wrong in speaking of Byzantines rather than Mongols: Mardin was 'was one of the Syrian fortresses facing the Byzantines. Its population was mixed: some Muslims and some Christians. The administration of it passed sometimes to the Byzantines, sometimes to the Muslims [...] Its inhabitants [...] found themselves at one time under the authority of the Muslims, and at another under the authority of the Christian Byzantines.'[1] Faraj mentions not only the Tatars but also the Jews, no doubt prompted by what Ibn Taymiyya wrote about Rashīd al-Dīn

---

1 Mardin had been adjoined to the Islamic empire since 19/640; see V. Minorsky & C. E. Bosworth, *EI*[2] art. 'Mārdīn', 524.

Faḍl Allāh, the īlkhānid vizier of Jewish origin, or by Ibn Kathīr's (d. 774/1373) presentation of the *Yāsā*, the great legal code of Genghis Khan.[1] He prefers to turn it into ideology rather than history. Thus he makes a point of saying that 'the Tatars were governing by means of laws (*qānūn*) combining some elements of the Law (*sharīᶜa*) of the Jews and the Nazarenes, a part of Islam and a part of Jewish reasoning.' 'A land called Mardin had been governed according to the institutional regime (*ḥukm*) of Islam, subsequently power was taken over by people who implemented (*aqāma*) the institutional regime of unbelief.' Ideology again predominates in the minimal explication offered by ᶜAzzām of the historical context of the Mardin fatwa: it was a city that had used to be 'part of the domain of Islam, where the Legislation of God was implemented, and of which a group of unbelievers later made themselves masters, who reduced to nothing [therein] the Legislation of God.' As for the shaykhs al-Jarbūᶜ and al-Kibbī, they do not interest themselves in Mardin except in relation to the present time, with no concern at all for past history. For al-Jarbūᶜ, the land of Mardin 'whose situation was that determined by events' was a domain comparable to modern Arab countries. And al-Kibbī considers it as the 'land that was, in former times, the nearest to our present reality'. Alas, how little Ibn Baṭṭūṭa, the prince of Arab travellers, is read!

---

1 See, respectively, IBN TAYMIYYA, *Majmūᶜ al-fatāwā*, trans. MICHOT, 'Textes spirituels XII', 28–29, and 'Textes spirituels XIII', 26, n. 7.

It is only fair to note for the record that the historical account of certain Western 'specialists' in matters Islamic, who have taken an interest in the Mardin fatwa – albeit very different from that of the six readings presented here – has not been much better. I think, for example, of this recent text by Benjamin and Simon: '[…] in 1303 […] the Mamluk sultan ordered ibn Taymiyya to draft a fatwa that would justify a jihad against the Mongols, and then preach this message with all the fire he could summon in Cairo. The specific target of the fatwa was to be Muzaffar, the prince of Mardin, a fortified Arab city that guarded important trade routes in northern Mesopotamia. Muzaffar, a Muslim, served at the behest of Mongol overlords […] For ibn Taymiyya, the sultan's request was a perfect opportunity to put his thoughts into action. In his fatwa, he accused Muzaffar of ruling his Muslim subjects not according to sharia, Islamic law, but with infidel laws – the Yasa, the Mongol code of customary law that regulated personal status and set penalties for crimes – thus leading Muslims away from the faith. In short, ibn Taymiyya argued, Muzaffar had committed apostasy, a crime punishable by death. The fatwa served its purpose. The jihad against the Mongols was successful.'[1]

In point of fact, it has not been established that the three anti-Mongol fatwas of Ibn Taymiyya were commanded by the Mamlūk sultan al-Malik al-Nāṣir Muḥammad b. Qalāwūn, or that they date from 702/1303. Rather, some convin-

---

1 BENJAMIN & SIMON, *Age of Sacred Terror* (2002), 50–51. On Ibn Taymiyya and the *Yāsā*, see the anti-Mongol writings from *Majmūᶜ al-fatāwā*, trans. MICHOT, 'Textes spirituels XIII', 25–26.

cing elements in them incline one to link the most substantial of these fatwas to the Mongol project of invading Syria in 712/1313 (see below, p. 50, notes 1, 3). Besides, the name *Muẓaffar* does not appear either in these anti-Mongol fatwas or the Mardin fatwa. The king of Mardin, al-Malik *al-Muẓaffar* Qara Arslān, died in 691/1292, several years before the first invasion of Syria by Ghāzān in 699/1299. There is nothing to demonstrate that either he or his son Najm al-Dīn Ghāzī II, who reigned until 712/1312, had been 'the specific target' of any Taymiyyan fatwa whatever – not the Mardin fatwa, not the anti-Mongol fatwas, nor any others. In the fatwa of Mardin, no mention is made of prince, or king, or emir.

Perhaps Benjamin and Simon are not wholly responsible for the poverty of their scholarly knowledge of Islamic history – one may suspect that they were drawing on Gilles Kepel for a good part of their misinformation about the Mardin fatwa. Kepel – in keeping with his class dunce neo-orientalism and the breezy confidence (despite the rough and ready quality of his knowledge of Arabic[1]) for which he is known – has indeed no hesitation at all in presenting the fatwa of Mardin and/or the anti-Mongol fatwas of Ibn Taymiyya (the want of definiteness in the phrasing is typical) as a 'little known text which clearly designates the impious rulers of the city of Mardin and the Tatars as objects of jihād'.[2] Further, in respect of the 'rulers' of Mardin, Kepel

---

1 See, for example, MICHOT, 'Textes spirituels XIII', 26, n. 7
2 KEPEL, *Le Prophète et Pharaon*, 216; see also 250.

speaks[1] only of *al-Muẓaffar* Qara Arslān and of his father Najm al-Dīn Ghāzī I, not of his son Najm al-Dīn Ghāzī II, even though it was under the latter's reign that the īlkhānid attacks against Damascus, during which Ibn Taymiyya inspired the Syrian resistance, took place.[2]

---

1 *Ibid.*, 211.

2 In relation to the Mardin fatwa, it is also possible to turn up some gems of historical fabling in the Press. Consider the opening of this article by G. al-Maghlūth in the Saudi paper *al-Waṭan*: 'The majority of the militant movements that, in the Islamic world, consider themselves to be *salafī*, refer in their Legal positions to the fatwas of the Shaykh al-Islām [Ibn Taymiyya]. More particularly [they refer] to those that issued from him in the course of the wars of the Tatars with the Muslims, and whose objective was to fire up resistance to the Mongols (the Tatars), even though they [the Tatars] pretended to be Muslims. Among those of [Ibn Taymiyya's] views that contributed to the *fiqh* of the movements of struggle, there is the fact that, when the Tatars fortified themselves in the village of Mardin, he permitted to the elements [among the population who were] resisting the Tatars the destruction of the village with its inhabitants, [however] innocent. When it was said to him, "What is the fault of these innocents killed without having committed any crime or sin?", he said in reply: "On the Day of Resurrection, they will be restored to life in accordance with their intentions." ' (AL-MAGHLŪTH, 'Ibn Taymiyya… and the *fiqh* of killing', *al-Waṭan*, 498 (26 Dhū l-Qaᶜda 1422/ 9 February 2002)

Ibn Taymiyya mentions the ultimate fate of the innocent Muslims killed in the course of fighting with the Tatars in his third anti-Mongol fatwa (IBN TAYMIYYA, *Majmūᶜ al-fatāwā*, xxviii, 544–53). However, there is no linkage there, neither explicit nor implicit, with Mardin. As for the fatwa devoted to this city, no such question is raised in it at all. What we have

Returning to the six modern texts, the second observation one is bound to make is this: alike in respect of the concept of *hijra* and of the other major theme here – the concepts of domain of peace or domain of war – not one of the six authors deepens his reflection by turning to other texts by Ibn Taymiyya. It is as if, on these two issues, the Mardin fatwa to which they refer did not merit or did not need any intertextual clarification. Faraj's resort to the anti-Mongol fatwas, and the comparisons that some of the authors – ᶜAzzām and Sālim as well as Faraj – make between the position of the Damascene shaykh and the positions of some other great jurists of classical Islam cannot be considered as equivalent to such an intertextual enrichment, internal to the works of Ibn Taymiyya and related to the two themes mentioned.

Third observation: in both those authors who speak of it, namely shaykhs al-Jarbūᶜ and al-Kibbī, the *hijra* is not treated from the viewpoint of a fleeing from sin or from sinners. The ethical and spiritual dimensions that the theme carries in Ibn Taymiyya are missing.

The last observation, the one that will be the most significant for our purpose, is this: five of the authors – i.e., all of them except Shaykh al-Kibbī – who tackle the concepts of domain of Islam, domain of war, etc., adopt a political approach.

---

said above about its content and the Syrian raid against Mardin in 698/1299 suffice to confirm the fictitiousness of the whole of this story-telling, and the slanderous nature of the accusation laid against the Damascene theologian.

In fact the author of Text A, ʿAbd al-Salām Faraj, unquestioningly elides 'the institutions of Islam' (*aḥkām al-islām*) with 'Islamic government'. He further maintains that there is no difference between the Taymiyyan concept of domains of peace and war, as expounded in the Mardin fatwa, and those of Abū Ḥanīfa (d. 150/767) and of his disciples, Muḥammad b. al-Ḥasan al-Shaybānī (d. 189/805) and Abū Yūsuf Yaʿqūb al-Anṣārī (d. 182/798). For him, the reason for its being so is obvious: 'The status (*ḥukm*) of a domain follows from the institutions that govern it.' Thus, if those institutions are 'institutions of unbelief, it is a domain of unbelief'. And then, a State governed by the institutions of unbelief deserves war 'in spite of the fact that most of its inhabitants are Muslims'. It is a mystery to me how Faraj is able to consider this to be the position taken by Ibn Taymiyya in the Mardin fatwa, even though Ibn Taymiyya explicitly refuses therein to pronounce the Mesopotamian city as 'domain of war' for the reason that, to necessitate such a judgement, the inhabitants would have to be unbelievers. And that is without taking account of the fact that (as we have demonstrated above with reference to diverse texts) the Damascene theologian in general judges the status of a place to be a function of the conditions of the souls of its inhabitants. But Faraj, it would appear, has not read these other texts.

The reflections of ʿAzzām in Text B on the conditions for transition from the status of domain of Islam to that of domain of war have rather more depth than those of Faraj. His reasoning on the particular status of Afghanistan under Soviet occupation (1979–89) is, likewise, relatively well developed. In contrast to Faraj, Shaykh ʿAzzām distinguishes the third type of domain suggested by Ibn Taymiyya from the positions adopted by the great masters of classical *fiqh*. Also, he refuses to follow the opinions of contemporary Afghan ulema – for the majority of whom 'sovietized' Afghanistan remains a domain of Islam, while others judge it to have become a domain of war – and considers it a new 'Mardin', a place of composite status. That said, the way in which Shaykh ᶜAzzām approaches the theme of the status of domains and the way he reads the Mardin fatwa are, also, exclusively political. For him, 'the precise scale [to use] in order to know [the status of] a domain' is not, as with Ibn Taymiyya, the religious condition of its inhabitants, but 'the law (*qānūn*)'. The status of a domain is a function of the type of legislation, divine or human, put into effect by its rulers. And, just as for Faraj a State governed by the institutions of unbelief deserves war 'in spite of the fact that the most of its inhabitants are Muslims', for ᶜAzzām, if sovereignty belongs in a domain belongs to a law other than the *Sharīᶜa*, 'whatever this law may be, it is a domain of war; even when the inhabitants [thereof] are Muslims'.

Alternatively, Shaykh ᶜAzzām also says: 'Such a domain has ceased to be a domain of Islam but has not become a domain of war. It is a third [sort of] domain.' While he prefers in this way to resort to the example of Mardin, he nevertheless does not understand the unprecedented status that Ibn Taymiyya affirms for it except as a function of a political development signalled by a change in legislation and institutional system (*ḥukm*). For sure, he says not one word on the possible difference between the concept of 'institutions of Islam' (*aḥkām al-islām*), raised in the Mardin fatwa, and that of sovereignty of a legislation or government. Nor does he speak at all of the army (*jund*) mentioned by the theologian.

Mamlūk knight[1]

Developed though it is, the thought of Shaykh ᶜAzzām seems, to say it straightforwardly, rather confused, if not inconsistent, in its vacillation between the composite status

---

[1] From MS *BL Add. 18866* of AL-AQṢARAʾĪ, *Nihāyat al-suʾl wa-l-umniyya fī ᶜilm al-furūsiyya*, fol. 132[b] (773/1371). See REX SMITH, *Medieval Muslim Horsemanship* (1979), 26.

of Ibn Taymiyya and a general anathema in the manner of Faraj. One thing is clear, however, in either case: for him, to be a domain of Islam, or of composite status, or a domain of war, is basically a matter of institutions, of legislation, of governments, in short, of politics, not a matter of Muslims or unbelievers, of persons and souls. Thus, when he finally affirms a composite status for 'sovietized' Afghanistan, it is because 'some *institutions* of the domain of Islam and some *institutions* of the domain of war are implemented there', without any consideration at all of the Muslim character or otherwise of the people concerned. Though he appeals to his authority, ᶜAzzām is at a considerable remove from the reasons for which Ibn Taymiyya affirmed a third status for Mardin.

The analysis of the concept of domain of Islam offered by the Saudi dissident, al-Masᶜarī, in Text C, is markedly more elaborate than those of the two Islamist authors studied just above. So too is the use he makes in this regard of the Mardin fatwa. His point of departure is that a land or region's being Islamic does not suffice to constitute a domain of Islam. A land may be termed Islamic for the reason that it has a Muslim majority population, or for the reason that it constitutes a domain of Islam, or for its historical past, or for a range of other considerations. A land may nevertheless be an Islamic land and yet be, at the same time, a domain of unbelief. Indeed, for an Islamic land to be a domain of Islam two conditions must be met: that it is governed by Islam (*al-ḥukm bi-l-islām*) and that the security of life and property is guaranteed therein by 'the power of Islam'. Thus, al-Masᶜarī clarifies, a land conquered by Muslims ceases to be a domain of war and becomes a domain of Islam as and when it has an

Islamic government to guarantee its external and internal security, with no importance whatever accorded to whether the conquered population converts or remains unbelieving.

Without indicating what part of the Mardin fatwa he has in mind, al-Masʿarī calls attention to the distinction that Ibn Taymiyya applies 'between the characterization of the domain and the statuses of the persons of its inhabitants'. He does not, unfortunately, say any more about it. However, he does very pertinently gauge the significance of that bit of a sentence where the Damascene theologian speaks of an army of Muslims. His assumptions nevertheless prevent him from drawing out the better part of his intuitions and (in the end) he is in fact embarrassed by the Mardin fatwa – whence the reproach he addresses to Ibn Taymiyya that he was not 'accurate' (*daqīq*).

The reason is that, for the Saudi dissident, the concepts of 'institutions of Islam' (*aḥkām al-islām*), 'Islamic government' (*al-ḥukm bi-l-islām*) and 'Islamic power' (*sulṭān al-islām*) are confounded. Besides, the conditions to be met to be a domain of Islam are of a nature oriented exclusively to politics or security, with the logical consequence that 'the statuses of a domain and its characterizations are not necessarily the statuses of its inhabitants or the characterization [that one gives] to them'. It would be difficult to imagine an approach more manifestly contrary to the perspective of Ibn Taymiyya. So one wonders why al-Masʿarī persists in wanting to appeal to his authority, and one understands why such an ideological balancing act would be at times a cause of trouble to him.

The author of Text D, Shaykh ʿAbd al-ʿAzīz al-Jarbūʿ, is also relatively troubled by the composite status affirmed for

Mardin by Ibn Taymiyya. The Mesopotamian city seems to him a sort of medieval prefiguring of modern Arab countries, whose 'populace are Muslim all together' and whose 'institutional system is apostate'. Then, '[t]here can be no doubt that the status of such a domain [is that it] is no longer Muslim'. Or, as he also writes, for an eye that is not in the least deceived by appearances, the 'unbelief is manifest' in such a domain.

That is to say, Shaykh al-Jarbūᶜ is personally inclined to see, in such an Arab country, a domain of unbelief. Nevertheless, his respect for Ibn Taymiyya's exertion of mental effort (*ijtihād*) on the status of Mardin constrains him to entertain the notion that such a country may also be of composite status. A minimal concession, as he hastens to add that, in all events, as regards the obligation to emigrate from such a country (for one unable openly to practise Islam therein), the difference between the statuses of domain of unbelief or composite domain is merely verbal (*lafẓī*)!

How might one judge the Saudi Islamist as one faithful to the Mamlūk theologian? As was indicated above, to have a domain of unbelief and of war, according to Ibn Taymiyya, it is a condition that the inhabitants themselves be unbelievers. Now, it is plain that Shaykh al-Jarbūᶜ has no care or concern other than about the nature of the systems of government and institutions. In politicizing in this way the thought of the master to whose authority he appeals, he is less near to him than to a Faraj, an ᶜAzzām or an al-Masᶜarī.

None of the four Islamist writers studied thus far questions the relevance for our epoch of the distinction domain of Islam/domain of unbelief or war. The author of Text E, the Syrian intellectual and London resident, Z. Sālim, considers that distinction to be outdated. He offers as proof that Ibn Taymiyya himself was not satisfied with it and so introduced the concept of a domain of the composite sort. Such a distinction was relative to a particular historical situation, to a particular conjunction of circumstances. Holding to it now is 'a strategic blunder and, vis-à-vis the Law, a major error'. As for holding to it, claiming that many modern Muslim countries are a part of the domain of war, and initiating a war against them, this is 'forbidden by the Law'. Sālim thus calls on contemporary Muslim jurists to re-examine the former distinctions and to propose others better fitted to our epoch, and in so doing to take the road of wisdom, for 'a good word [placed] in a good heart is a thousand times better than stray bullets fired from here and there.'

There we have Ibn Taymiyya knowingly put at the service of a 'progressivist' cause. But, in respect of what, according to him, is the proper ground of the status of a domain, his thought is hardly better understood for that, since Sālim shares the politicizing perspective common to the four authors mentioned earlier, albeit with an insistence on the security aspect, in which he is closer to al-Masʿarī, with perhaps also a little more attention to the strictly religious aspects of the *Sharīʿa.* Thus, according to Sālim, the historical distinction domain of Islam/domain of war has two bases: 'security, and the nature of the regime in power, [determined] according to the public practice of the rites and the implementation of the prescriptions'. In other words, '[t]he domain of Islam is not only the one where most of the inhabitants are Muslims; and the domain of unbelief is not only the one where most of the inhabitants are unbelievers.'

What then, once more, of a Taymiyyan statement like, for example, this one: 'The statuses of regions change by virtue of the change in the situations of their inhabitants. A region may be a domain of unbelief when its inhabitants are unbelievers. It then becomes a domain of Islam when its inhabitants become Muslims'?

As much as Sālim puts us on guard against an ill-considered use of the distinction between domains of Islam, of war, etc., the author of the last text (F), the Lebanese shaykh Saᶜd al-Dīn al-Kibbī, criticizes whoever calls too readily to jihād, without respecting the conditions that classical *fiqh* insists upon for the conduct of war, among them the capacity to wage it. In his opinion, the obligation to fight is not absolute, unconditional, and he offers as proof that Ibn Taymiyya, in the Mardin fatwa, makes emigration obligatory or preferable for the weak who are unable to practise Islam publicly.

The Mardin fatwa used as a brake on an excessive jihādism – that is something too striking to let pass unremarked. At very least it proves (as indeed does what Sālim said of this fatwa) that several readings of it are possible. It is well to remember also the relative difficulty into which, at one point, this Taymiyyan text plunged al-Masᶜarī and Shaykh al-Jarbūᶜ…

AN UNFAITHFUL POSTERITY

Five of the six modern texts discussed above take up the fatwa of Mardin for the concepts of domain of Islam, domain of war, etc., and they have in common an essentially political reading of it. The clarification of this fatwa provided in the first part of this Introduction by referring to other writings of the Mamlūk theologian makes it at least difficult to regard such a reading as faithful to the thought expressed in the fatwa, whose particularly juridical–religious, ethical and person-oriented character has been amply underlined.[1]

---

[1] Whereas five of the six modern authors studied above who refer to the Mardin fatwa are not faithful to him, Ibn Taymiyya would probably feel himself to be quite close to cyber-muftis like the shaykhs ᶜA. Saqr and F. Mawlawi when, albeit without citing him, they speak of the domains of Islam, of war, or of unbelief, as follows:

'Muslim scholars maintain that the labeling of a country or place as being an Islamic country or a non-Islamic one, Dār al-Ḥarb, revolves around the question of religious security. This means that if a Muslim practices Islam freely in his place of abode despite that the place happens to be secular or un-Islamic, then he will be considered as living in a Dār al-Islām, meaning that he is not obliged to [e]migrate from that place.' (SAQR, *Concept of Dar al-Islam and Dar al-Harb*, 2002)

'Any country is a domain of Islam where there is a Muslim majority, even if its ruler is not someone who fully observes Islam, and even if his government deploys certain types of anti-Islamic arrangements or policy. On the other hand, any country which has a non-Muslim majority will be regarded as a domain of unbelief.' (MAWLAWI, *Dar al-Kufr: An Abode of Daᶜwah, not War*, 2002)

What most clearly distinguishes these two shaykhs from the Damascene theologian is their interest in propagating Islam by *daᶜwa*, by missionary action – something quite normal, given the relatively recent character of this effort in the Sunnī world (see P. Walker, R. Schulze, M. Masud, *OEMIW* art. 'Daᶜwah').

'The injunction of making *hijra* from *dār al-kufr* to *dār al-Islām* is still pending and will remain so up to the Day of Judgement.

However, is it an obligation or is it just a recommended act? Scholars say: if a Muslim is afraid for his religion and ethics, or for his property, then it is a duty for him to emigrate, otherwise the emigration is merely a *Sunnah* for him. Yet scholars also point out that if a Muslim finds that by remaining in *dār al-kufr* he will be a source of help for Muslims in *dār al-Islām* or will be helping the Muslims in *dār al-kufr*, by teaching them religion or propagating Islam itself by spreading its principles and answering questions about it, and correcting people's misconceptions about it, then it is better for him to stay in that society, rather than leave it. However, this requires the Muslim to have strong faith, a strong personality, and the means that will enable him to carry out this mission. In the dawn of Islam, preachers and traders played a major role in spreading Islam in non-Muslim countries.' (SAQR, *Concept of Dar al-Islam and Dar al-Harb*, 2002)

'As we see in Muslim countries, Muslim *du*ʿ*āt* (callers to Islam) aim at reforming the systems and exhorting the government so that they will completely abide by the Islamic teachings, whereas in non-Muslim countries they aim at spreading the Islamic message among non-Muslims so as to convince them to embrace Islam. It's a fact that some Muslims regard every non-Muslim country as an abode of war, *dār al-ḥarb*, basing this on the opinions of some jurists who were greatly influenced by certain historical circumstances. In my opinion, this is not true, for the general rule regarding the abode of disbelief is that they should be regarded originally as an abode of *da*ʿ*wa* (calling to Islam) not of war. But they may turn into an abode of war under certain circumstances and within certain conditions.' (MAWLAWI, *Dar al-Kufr: An Abode of Da*ʿ*wah, not War*, 2002)

According to Tariq RAMADAN (*Être Musulman Européen*, 205; *Dār ash-shahāda*, 25; *Les Musulmans d'Occident*, 117), 'the juristic opinion current' among the ulema of the classical period, namely that 'the domain of Islam must be the abode of the

It is important to pause a moment over this judgement of unfaithfulness in order properly to gauge its entail and its gravity.[1]

According to Kepel, whether various Islamists, who in the manner of Faraj, claimed to have found in the works of Ibn Taymiyya 'the reference in the Muslim Tradition that they were seeking in order to give their action a legal basis [...] did or did not distort the texts is a question that is asked by actors on the contemporary Egyptian scene who, these and those, arrogate to themselves the monopoly in interpretation, canonical or "modernist", of the great traditionist.'[2] Far be it from me to arrogate to myself here any monopoly whatever, or to strive, through an exercise in interpretation that could never amount to anything but a poor second line of defence, to impose 'my' Ibn Taymiyya.[3] The more so as, in allowing Ibn Taymiyya to speak for himself through a series of texts that complement and confirm each other, I

Muslims where the Islamic legal system is applied (even if some non-Muslims have taken power)' was 'also held by Ibn Taymiyya'. The intertextual study of the Mardin fatwa presented in this work would not seem to permit such a summary of the Damascene theologian's position.

1 To prevent any misunderstanding, I stress that the unfaithfulness discussed here is to a thought, not the infidelity of unbelief. I anathematize no-one. How otherwise, religiously speaking, not share the concerns and the struggles of some of the authors studied?

2 KEPEL, *Le Prophète et Pharaon*, 216; also SIVAN, 'Ibn Taymiyya: Father of the Islamic Revolution', 41; *Radical Islam*, 103–04, 107; JĀD AL-ḤAQQ, *Kutayb al-farīḍat al-ghāʾiba wa-l-radd ʿalay-hi.*

3 KEPEL, *Intellectuels et militants de l'islam contemporain*, 20–22.

did not have to interpret him but could be content to read him. Thus my approach has been essentially philological and historical. In some ways it has indeed been a kind of monkish toil, for lack of which (we may be permitted to suppose) no small number of more or less extremist activisms, and flashy neo-orientalist studies, socio-religious or theologico-political, may well be found wanting.

That said, one can agree that the result obtained is far from disappointing. Rather than a distortion of the Mardin fatwa, what has been confirmed in respect of Faraj, ᶜAzzām, al-Masᶜarī, Shaykh al-Jarbūᶜ and Sālim, is a fundamental misconstruction of its meaning. Between them and Ibn Taymiyya there has thus opened a wide and deep gap of wrong understanding.

Not long ago I had wondered[1] how authentically what I then called a 'Mongolizing' Islamism was attributed to Ibn Taymiyya in that his anti-Mongol fatwas were being exploited to call to an armed rebellion against the rulers or governments of certain modern Muslim countries, those rulers having being identified with the medieval Tatars. I here confirm that to use the writings of Ibn Taymiyya in this way to 'Mongolize' the governments of certain present-day Muslim countries is indeed to betray his thought.[2] His principal anti-

---

1 MICHOT, 'Textes spirituels XI', 28.

2 I must clarify that to speak of a betrayal by 'Mongolizing' Islamism of the thought of Ibn Taymiyya does not constitute a judgement on the legitimacy or illegitimacy, in terms of the religion, of the struggle of this form of Islamism or of the means used to wage it. That is quite another question that requires taking into account a number of other parameters,

Mongol fatwa, dating more or less certainly from the years 709–712/1310–1313, was in fact a text for a mobilization against a foreign invader. The dangerousness of that non-Arab invader was affirmed by and well known to the theologian, who had experience of it from his childhood on.[1] Further, the invader's attachment to Islam was, for Ibn Taymiyya, that much more suspect, not only for having been relatively recent, but also because the successor of the īlkhān Ghāzān, Öljāytū (r. 703–17/1304–17), had then become Shīʿī.[2] The radicalism of Ibn Taymiyya's anti-Mongol writings needs to be understood as a function of these factors, whose importance cannot be overstated.[3]

---

and about which I do not take it upon myself to pronounce in this work. Here, I am doing nothing more that inviting 'Mongolizing' Islamism to contrive for itself some other canonical patronage than that of the Damascene theologian.

1 Ibn Taymiyya had direct contact with the Mongols at the time of their invasions of Syria in 699/1299–1300 and 702/1303. See MICHOT, *Lettre à un roi croisé*, 74–82. He could also have been informed about them by his brother Zayn al-Dīn, whose business affairs took him in particular to Tabrīz in 694/1295: see MELVILLE, 'Pādishāh-i Islām: the Conversion of Ghāzān to Islām' (1990).

2 On the dating of this fatwa, the (for Ibn Taymiyya) doubtful nature of Mongol Islam, and the conversion of Öljāytū to Shīʿism, see IBN TAYMIYYA, *Majmūʿ al-fatāwā*, trans. MICHOT, 'Textes spirituels XI–XIII', esp. 'XI', 27 and 'XII', 30, n. 36.

3 It was observed earlier (see above, p. 25 and note 1) that anti-Mongolism perhaps has some part in Ibn Taymiyya's refusal to accord to Mardin the status of domain of peace. That said, the difference in tone between the Mardin fatwa and the anti-Mongol fatwas is plain. In the most substantive of those fatwas, the Syrian Shaykh al-Islām judges it obligatory to fight

against those who abstain from giving rulings 'according to that by which the Book and the Tradition give rulings'. The issue for him was mobilizing against a foreign invader, whence the emphatic and intransigent quality of his argument. In the fatwa on Mardin, he likewise mentions, indirectly, the absence in this city of implementation of the institutions of Islam (in the sense indicated above, pp. 19–20, and notes 1–2). But he does not then go any further than refusing to it the status of domain of peace. He does not make it a domain of war, against which hostilities might be unleashed. He is content, rather than call for any kind of general mobilization, to invite us to consider the situation as a function of individual persons: 'the Muslim shall be treated as he merits and [...] the one who departs from the Way/Law of Islam shall be combated as he merits.' In fact, the tone of the Mardin fatwa does not come as near that of the anti-Mongol fatwas as it does that of the extract (translated below), in which, inviting once again to balanced reflection and perhaps thinking of the īlkhān Ghāzān, he prefers not to denounce the drunkenness of a king but newly converted to Islam. Must one conclude that Ibn Taymiyya modulates and (in the negative sense) makes a tool of the religion, fitting it to whatever objectives he is pursuing, sometimes mobilizing people, sometimes calming them down? Here, let me recall two judicious observations of Henri Laoust: 'The works of Ibn Taymiyya, written day by day under the influence of events, are responsive to the circumstances that motivate and explain them' (LAOUST, *Essai sur les doctrines*, 486). And: 'It does not seem that one should [...] give to the thought of Ibn Taymiyya a more pronounced systematization than he himself gave to it. His teaching often depends on the needs of his polemic, and the need to adapt the Law to circumstances means that even the theoretical conditions for excommunication can be a function of time and place' (*ibid.*, 263). To this I would add that the Damascene theologian did not act in this way except that, as he explains also in the following text, he wished to be true to the Prophet whose positions varied in light of situations:

'When one knows that [certain people], to whom one might prohibit these evil deeds, will then abandon certain [other] deeds whose goodness is preponderant [and which are] obligatory, they will not be prohibited from them – given what such a prohibition might entail, [through] the abandonment of the obligatory good deeds, as a factor of corruption – unless it is possible to reconcile the two things, in which case the whole of what is obligatory will be accomplished. Thus ʿUmar b. al-Khaṭṭāb employed someone in [the behaviour of] whom there was depravity, given the preponderance of the interest that his work presented; then, by his own strength and justice, he made him cease his depravity.

'Then, to abstain from prohibiting evil deeds, will be like abstaining from reprimanding [an evil] by hand or by arms when there may be in so doing a factor of corruption preponderant over the corruptive character of that which was to be reprimanded. When prohibiting has, in a particular affair, as a necessary concomitant of it, the abandonment of something whose commended quality (*maʿrūf*) is preponderant, that is equivalent to having as a necessary concomitant the accomlishment of something whose reprehensible quality (*munkar*) is preponderant. Thus it is for one who converts to Islam on condition of praying only two prayers, as is related of someone who converted in the time of the Prophet, the prayer of God be upon him and may He give him peace. So too it is for one of the kings who, having received his power [from God], converts to Islam but drinks wine or does certain [other] things, against which there is an interdiction. If that were prohibited to him, he might apostasize from Islam.

'There is a difference, for scholar or emir, between [on the one hand] the act of abstaining from prohibiting a thing to certain people when prohibiting it entails a preponderant element of corruption, and, on the other hand, the act of authorizing them to commit it. This varies as situations vary, and in

By contrast, when the theologian expressed himself on the internal policy of the Egyptian–Syrian sultanate, to whose jurisdiction he belonged, his discourse was of an altogether different character. Although the Mamlūks in Cairo exercised power in a way that, from the viewpoint of the religion, could be subject to serious reserve or criticism, he commended patience above all. To be sure, just as the Prophet said: 'There is no obedience to any creature in disobedience to the Creator'. And moreover, we are also commanded by the Prophet 'to speak – or take up the cause of – the Truth wherever we may be, without fearing, in respect of God, blame from anyone.' That said, in the face of the injustice

---

another situation, the prohibition will have to be made public, either so that the prohibition [of the thing] may be evident and one is thereby convinced of it and fearful of committing it, or in the hope that it will be abandoned, or as an expression of indignation – according to the situations. It is for that reason that the positions [adopted by] the Prophet, the prayer of God be upon him and may He give him peace, were of diverse kinds, whether it was a question for him of enjoining or prohibiting, of waging jihād or pardoning, [or when] implementing penalties, of being strict or merciful.' (IBN TAYMIYYA, *Majmū*ᶜ *al-fatāwā*, xxxv. 31–32)

An interesting case of setting an important interdiction of the religion to one side, out of concern to avoid a greater evil, is reported about Ghāzān. Barely converted to Islam, the īlkhān threatened to apostasize if he was not permitted to wed the widow of his deceased father. Aware of the gravity of such an abandonment of Islam by the Mongol king of Persia, a shaykh permitted to him this twisting of the Islamic Law. See AMITAI-PREISS, 'Ghāzān, Islām, and Mongol Tradition: A View from the Mamlūk Sultanate' (1996), 3.

and oppression of rulers, it is patience that is obligatory, and it is not permitted to engage in sedition against them. The Prophet said: 'Whoever sees in his emir a thing that he detests, let him be patient in regard to it! Whoever separates himself by a span from the community of the believers and then dies, his death is that of a man of the age of Ignorance.'

Ibn Taymiyya invites us, in short, to be mindful of how (according to the *Ṣaḥīḥ*s of al-Bukhārī and Muslim) ʿUbāda b. al-Ṣāmit and others gave their pledge of allegiance to the Prophet: 'We have pledged allegiance to God's Messenger, may God bless him and give him peace, undertaking the following commitments: to listen and obey when that is easy for us and when that is hard for us, when we feel like it and when the thing is repugnant to us, preferring [the doing of] it to ourselves; not to dispute the authority of those who hold it; to speak – or take up the cause of – the Truth wherever we may be; not to have fear, in respect of God, of the blame of anyone.'

In the Cairo prison where he was unjustly locked up, in 706/1307, after a trial as iniquitous as it was expeditious, Ibn Taymiyya commented on this tradition about allegiance, seeing in it 'three fundamentals combining everything: to obey within obedience to God, even if the one giving the order is unjust; to abstain from disputing the authority of those who dispose it; to take up the cause of the Truth without fear of any creature.'[1]

---

1 IBN TAYMIYYA, *Majmūʿ al-fatāwā*, trans. MICHOT, 'Textes spirituels X', 29–30 (wherein references to the ḥadīths cited here). On 'the political loyalty' and 'the critical obedience' of

Ibn Taymiyya, see: LAOUST, *Essai sur les doctrines*, 310–15, 'Le réformisme d'Ibn Taimīya' (1962), 41–42; CARRÉ, *Mystique et politique: Lecture révolutionnaire du Coran par Sayyid Quṭb* (1984), 21 n. 1. On his patriotism, see MICHOT, 'Textes spirituels XI', 27; 'XIII', 26–28; the letter to the sultan al-Nāṣir trans. in *Rashīd al-Dīn*, 134–35. On the typology within which the Damascene shaykh arranges the different Legitimate kinds of recourse to force, his fundamental condemnation of violence between Muslims, and his refusal of any blind obedience to power as well as of every insurrection against it, see the very useful synthesis of K. ABOU EL FADL, *Rebellion and Violence in Islamic Law* (2001), 271–79. See also the two types of 'enemies of God departing from the religion' that Ibn Taymiyya distinguishes in his letter to al-Nāṣir, trans. MICHOT, *Rashīd al-Dīn*, 135.

SIVAN ('Ibn Taymiyya: Father of the Islamic Revolution', 44; *Radical Islam*, 99–100) and JANSEN (*De radicaal-islamitische ideologie: van Ibn Taymiyya tot Osama ben Laden* [2004], 7) rightly question the reasons for Ibn Taymiyya's argument for loyalty towards the Mamlūk sultans. However, in their explanation for it – namely, in the main, the Mamlūks' successes in jihād against the Mongols and the Crusaders – they attach too little importance to the part played by the religion itself in the theologian's quietism, whether in respect of the conditions of allegiance to the Prophet or in the Ḥanbalī tradition on the matter.

JANSEN (*De radicaal-islamitische ideologie*) does not raise the question of how authentically 'Mongolizing' Islamism is attributed to Ibn Taymiyya. SIVAN ('Ibn Taymiyya: Father of the Islamic Revolution', 42; *Radical Islam*, 99) does raise it but quickly drops it again. Both of them are in fact much more interested in this contemporary Islamism than in the medieval theologian. Relaying above all else the Islamist reading of Ibn Taymiyya, without so much of genuine critical spirit as to investigate appropriately the corpus of his work, they legitimize in some degree that

Whatever the reasons for it – a strict fidelity to the Messenger, a pragmatic morality opting for the lesser evil (of the sort that informs Texts III and IV), or, rather more likely (given the manner of acting of the Prophet himself), the two combined – the non-violent quietism of Ibn Taymiyya vis-à-vis the power on which he depended is an undeniable fact. On the hypothesis (itself subject to discussion[1]) that some medieval texts might be used to understand and dictate to the present, this quietism suffices to forbid any transposition of his fatwas on mobilization against the Mongols from the domain of foreign affairs or defence against an external enemy to the domain of internal politics. And then, how should we fail to recall here the profound reservations the theologian expresses, at the end of Text IV, about any hasty, ill-considered generalization from the judgements of the Prophet or from the opinions of the ulema?

This clarification on the betrayal of the thought of Ibn Taymiyya by 'Mongolizing' Islamism was necessary so that the unfaithfulness for which I reproach Faraj, ᶜAzzām, al-Masᶜarī, al-Jarbūᶜ and Sālim should not be identified with it. That infidelity is indeed of a different nature in this respect that it holds, neither more nor less, to the political accent in their approach to the Mardin fatwa. It is situated at a much deeper hermeneutic level therefore than that of an extremist

---

reading at the expense of non-Islamist readings, 'official' or otherwise. This practical collusion between 'Mongolizing' Islamism and a certain Orientalism merits a study to itself; see below, pp. 123–128 and notes.

1 See MICHOT, *Ibn Taymiyya. Le Statut des moines* (1997), 18–19; *Ibn Taymiyya. Le Haschich et l'extase* (2001), 63–64.

reading that proceeds by a Mongolization of the State or according to any other form of incitement to armed insurrection against it.[1]

That contemporary Islamist debate should be essentially political is normal, particularly in its engagement with certain modern Muslim States.[2] The transposition into the past of concepts of the State, of institutional regime, of political system, and other a priori forms of the modern understanding of the collective life of societies, such as has been observed in our five authors, should not therefore surprise us overmuch. It nevertheless remains to ask if such a transposition is pertinent. In other words, is the thinking of Ibn Taymiyya, in the Mardin fatwa and the other of his texts here taken into account, really a political thinking? Whether in respect of the concept of *hijra* or the concepts of domain of Islam, domain of war, etc., the intertextual approach to the Mardin fatwa pursued above necessitates a negative response

---

1 Even before it betrays Ibn Taymiyya by Mongolization, the Islamism of a Faraj is already unfaithful to him by its politicization. The betrayal here presupposes the unfaithfulness but the latter does not automatically imply a betrayal. The Islamism that appeals to the authority of Ibn Taymiyya can also politicize him without Mongolizing, as is the case for example with ʿAzzām.

2 It remains to be asked – but this is not the objective of this work – if this politicization of contemporary Islamist debate, however normal in this modern period, perpetuates its passive Westernization or is its best guarantee of success. That Islam is *dīn wa-dawla* could mean, not that it *must be* 'religion and State' but that it *take the place of*, at the same time, the one and the other.

to that question. The construction that our five authors give to this fatwa thus commits the sin of anachronistic projecttion.

Without, to be sure, passing from one extreme to the other – in this case from politicizing to being a-political – it may be worthwhile to ask, in the light of the intertextual study of the Mardin fatwa, about the general categorization, prevalent today, of Ibn Taymiyya as a political thinker. I mean as a thinker about the State, about the organization and exercise in a society of civil power as a function of the integrated whole of laws and human institutions – in this particular case, about a system of government claiming the legacy of Greek political philosophy, which was more or less well-known in the classical Arab-Muslim world and which, to this day, has held a considerable paradigmatic value.

Thoroughly informed as he was about 'ideal city' projects like those of an al-Fārābī or of the Ancients, Ibn Taymiyya openly mocked the political pretensions of the philosophers. Thus, he did not hesitate to write, of Aristotle: 'Have you ever seen a philosopher who might have improved the well-being of a single village? To say nothing of [improving] a city?!'[1] Further, when he wished to give an example of rule by princes (*siyāsa malakiyya*) 'appealing [for authority or guidance] neither to a confession nor to a Book' – in short, 'rational' (*ʿaqlī*) – it is Genghis Khan that he thought of,

---

1 See IBN TAYMIYYA, *Darʾ al-taʿāruḍ*, trans. MICHOT, 'A Mamlūk Theologian's Commentary on Avicenna's *Risāla Aḍḥawiyya*' (2003), Part II, 339.

rather than of Plato or Aristotle.[1] Instead of presupposing that the Damascene theologian was reflecting, in the Mardin fatwa, or indeed even in his *Siyāsa sharʿiyya*, as a political thinker or theoretician of the State, it would surely be more useful to give, first of all, their full weight to the lineaments of his scholarly persona – religion, jurisprudence (*fiqh*), ethics, the spiritual life of the souls – which are known beyond doubt because textually evident. So too, it would be more useful to give its due weight to the historical context in which he lived. Perhaps even Laoust, in his master work on Ibn Taymiyya, tended to speak a little too much of the State.

One can readily imagine the implications of such questions and hypotheses in the face of the claims of the advocates of the creation of Islamic States who appeal, in this age, to the authority of the Shaykh al-Islām. What could there be of advantage, to supply the current political debate from within, in a thinker moving, in his medieval vision of society, between the authority of the ulema and the military power of the Mamlūk emirs? Let us turn back to this striking passage from the Mardin fatwa, speaking of a 'domain of peace in which the institutions of Islam are implemented, because its army is [composed of] Muslims'.

If such a passage is political and holds its relevance for our epoch, does one not court the risk that the only thing that the Mardin fatwa might serve to legitimize is the existence of the contemporary Middle-Eastern military regimes,

---

1 See IBN TAYMIYYA, *Majmūʿ al-fatāwā*, trans. MICHOT, 'Textes XIV', 26. See also Ibn Taymiyya's affirmation (below, p. 77 n.) that the Turks, meaning the Mongols, 'do not fight for religion'.

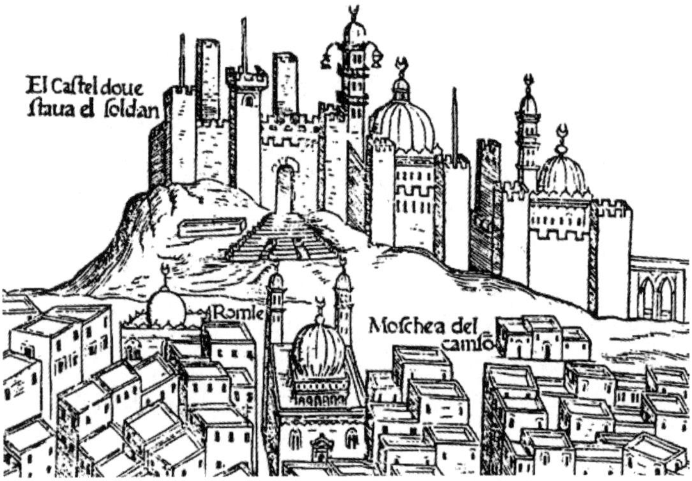

The citadel of the Mamlūk sultans in Cairo[1]

sometimes labelled as 'neo-Mamlūk'? If, on the other hand, this text has no value except in relation to its own time and except that the institutions mentioned in it must be understood only from the viewpoint of religion, will it not be judged, relatively to modern times, as incurably obsolete and outdated? If, in the end, this text is considered as the expression of a thought unconnected to circumstances, of a juridical–religious nature, and which wishes itself nourished exclusively by the Qur'ān, by the Tradition of the Prophet, by the example of the pious ancestors of the Community, etc., and which, through the implementation of the institutions of the *Sharīʿa* under the protection of an army of Muslims, suggests

---

1 From G. D. ZORZI, *Descritione* (*c.* 1500).

an atemporal paradigm, will one ever be able to see politics in it, or a thought about the State, in the sense usually given to these words? That does not imply that such a model is to be excluded on principle, but at most that it would be helpful to find an appropriate name for it.

The moment has come to call a halt to these musings. The more so as – if I may be permitted to admit it – the point of departure for this present work was not the Mardin fatwa but Text II: I translated it first, before all the others that may be read below, in the course of research into the Taymiyyan concept of *hijra*. Having set out thus, I in fact arrived at a turn-around of the thematic priorities, which has led me here. I will surely be excused the inconstancy of this migration from one topic to another since Ibn Taymiyya himself allows that, in function of the conditions of souls, a mosque may become a tavern, and vice versa… And could it not be that, besides their anachronistic politicization of the Mardin fatwa, Faraj, ᶜAzzām, al-Masᶜarī, al-Jarbūᶜ and Sālim have missed all that the Taymiyyan treatment of the issues of *hijra*, of the domains of war and of Islam, of unbelief and of faith, holds of great interest for a modern Muslim spirituality?

The four texts of Ibn Taymiyya at the centre of the present work were read in the edition of them given by ᶜAbd al-Raḥmān b. Muḥammad b. Qāsim in his *Majmūᶜ al-fatāwā* (Collected fatwas of Ibn Taymiyya). Text I is in vol. xxviii, pp. 240–41 (line 5); Text II in vol. xviii, pp. 279 (line 12)–84; Text III is in vol. xxviii, pp. 216–17 (line 3); Text IV is in vol. xxviii, pp. 210 (line 4)–13. The headings and sub-headings have been added by the translator.

'Power to our master, the Sultan! …'
Escutcheon of the Mamlūk sultan al-Nāṣir Muḥammad
b. Qalāwūn (beginning of the eighth/fourteenth century)

Texts of Ibn Taymiyya

I. FLEE MARDIN?

[Ibn Taymiyya], God have mercy on him, was questioned about the land of Mardin. Is it a land of war (*balad ḥarb*) or a land of peace (*balad silm*)? Does a Muslim resident therein have a duty to emigrate [do *hijra*] to the lands of Islam or not? If emigration is obligatory for him and he does not emigrate, and he gives assistance to the enemies of the Muslims with his person or his goods, is he sinning in so [doing]? And one who accuses him of hypocrisy (*nifāq*) and insults him [by calling him a hypocrite], is he sinning or not?

He answered: All praise is due to God!

There is an interdiction against (*muḥarram*) [any assault on] the lives and property of Muslims wherever they may be, in Mardin or anywhere else.

To give assistance to those who depart from the Way/Law of the religion of Islam (*sharīʿa*) is also forbidden, whether it be the people of Mardin or others.

If the one resident [in Mardin] is disabled from putting his religion into effect (*iqāma*), it is obligatory for him to emigrate. If that is not [the case], it [remains] preferable [but] is not obligatory.

That [these people] give assistance to the enemy of the Muslims with their persons or their property is forbidden to them, and they must abstain therefrom by all the means possible to them – evading, equivocating, compromising.[1] When it is not possible for them to do this except by emigrating, [emigrating] is incumbent on every single one of them.

It is not lawful to insult them in a general manner, nor to accuse them of hypocrisy [hiding unbelief]. Rather, insulting and accusing of hypocrisy is to be done in respect of the specific characteristics mentioned in the Book and the *Sunna*.[2] Now this concerns the people of Mardin and others also.

---

1 'In transactions (*muʿāmala*) with the Tatars, that is permitted which is permitted with those like them, and that is forbidden which is forbidden with those like them. It is permitted that one buy from them their dyed (*muwashshā*) fabrics, their horses, etc., just as one buys dyed fabrics from the Bedouin, the Turkomans, and Kurds, as also their horses. Of foodstuffs, clothes, etc., one is permitted to sell to them that which it is permitted to sell to those like them. As for selling to them, to them and to other than them, such things as would assist them in committing forbidden acts – for example, to sell horses and armaments to someone who will use them to engage in forbidden [acts and forms of] fighting – this is not permitted. God, – Exalted is He – has said [Qurʾān, *al-Māʾida*, 5. 2]: "Help one another in piety and fear [of God]. Do not help one another in sin and hostility. And fear God! God is assuredly severe in [His] punishment." ' (IBN TAYMIYYA, *al-Masāʾil al-Mārdīniyya*, 141; *Majmūʿ al-fatāwā*, xxix. 275. See also LAOUST, *Essai sur les doctrines*, 368, n. 1.)

2 Even insult and accusation of hypocrisy must obey the rules defined by the religion, rather than being left to individual discretion: see IBN TAYMIYYA, *al-Siyāsat al-sharʿiyya*, trans. LAOUST, *Le traité de droit public d'Ibn Taymīya*, 217–21; IBN NAQĪB AL-

Is [Mardin] a domain of war or of peace? It is a [city of a status] composite (*murakkab*), in which both the things signified [by those terms are to be found]. It is not in the situation of a domain of peace in which the institutions (*aḥkām*) of Islam are implemented because its army (*jund*) is [composed of] Muslims. Nor is it in the situation of a domain of war, whose inhabitants are unbelievers. Rather, it constitutes a third type [of domain], in which the Muslim shall be treated as he merits, and in which the one who departs from the Way/Law of Islam shall be combated as he merits.

Mardin
From a lithograph of NIEBUHR, *Voyage en Arabie et en d'autres pays circonvoisins* (1780), ii. Table xlvii

---

MIṢRĪ (d. 769/1368), *ʿUmdat al-sālik*, trans. KELLER, *Reliance of the Traveller* (1994), 686–87, 722; and see below, p. 69.

II. THE TRUE EMIGRANT

'The one whose *hijra*[1] is made to God and His Messenger, his *hijra* is made to God and His Messenger.'[2]

These words of [the Prophet] – may God pray over him and grant him peace – are not tautologous (*taḥṣīl li-l-ḥāṣil*), but inform [us] that, for one who has a certain intention in acting, that which is the object of his intention is realized. That is to say, the one whose *hijra* has as its objective (*qaṣada*) [going to] God and His Messenger, that which he has [in this way] as objective is realized for him. By contrast, the one whose objective is a *hijra* that is somewhat this-worldly, or [a *hijra* that] is [directed] to a woman, he obtains only that.[3]

---

1 'The *hijra*, in its apparent sense, is the travelling (*safar*) from one place to another. Now travelling is a genus comprising many species, which differ as a function of the intention of the traveller. It may be an obligatory journeying, like the pilgrimage or a jihād waged individually. It may also be something prohibited like the travelling of a highway robber or that of an oppressor attacking the community of the Muslims, of an escaping slave, or of a fugitive woman.' (IBN TAYMIYYA, *Majmū*ᶜ *fatāwā*, xviii. 253–54)

2 Extract from the hadith of intention: see the references given above, p. 12, n. 2.

3 'It is related that the reason for [which the Prophet made the statements reported in] this hadith is that a man had emigrated from Makka to Madina for a woman whom he loved, called Umm Qays. His *hijra* had been made for her sake and he was nicknamed *the emigrant of Umm Qays*.' IBN TAYMIYYA, *Majmū*ᶜ *al-fatāwā*, xviii. 253. On Ibn Taymiyya and women, see MICHOT,

That is a detailed exposition (*tafṣīl*) of his words: 'Deeds are valued only according to the[ir] intentions.' Having informed [us] that every man obtains that which he intends [to realize], he clarifies that the former obtains that which is the object of his intention, and the latter obtains that which is the object of his [intention].

THE PROPHET AND THE PROFOUND MEANING OF THINGS

Hijra is a derivative of *hajr*, 'to flee'. It is authentically reported from the Prophet – may God pray over him and grant him peace – that he said: 'The emigrant (*muhājir*) is the one who flees that which God has prohibited.[1] The warrior (*mujāhid*) is the one who fights against himself for the sake of God (*fī dhāt Allāh*).[2] [Just] as he said [also]: 'The Muslim (*muslim*) is the one from whose tongue and hand the Muslims are safe (*salima*).[3] The believer (*mu'min*) is the one before whom the

---

'Un célibataire endurci et sa maman: Ibn Taymiyya (d. 728/1328) et les femmes' (2001).

1 See AL-BUKHĀRĪ, *Ṣaḥīḥ*, *Īmān*, i. 11 (*ʿĀlam*. 9); IBN ḤANBAL, *Musnad*, ii. 192 (*ʿĀlam*. 6515).

2 See IBN ḤANBAL, *Musnad*, vi. 21, 22 (*ʿĀlam*. 22833, 22842); AL-TIRMIDHĪ, *Sunan*, *Faḍā'il al-jihād*, iii. 89, no. 1671 (*ʿĀlam*. 1546). On the phrase *fī dhāt Allāh*, see IBN TAYMIYYA, *Dar' al-taʿāruḍ*, trans. MICHOT, 'A Mamlūk Theologian's Commentary', Part II, 330: 'for the sake of God, that is to say on the path of God and going towards Him.'

3 See AL-BUKHĀRĪ, *Ṣaḥīḥ*, *Īmān*, i. 11 (*ʿĀlam*. 9); IBN ḤANBAL, *Musnad*, vi. 21, 22 (*ʿĀlam*. 22833, 22842).

people feel themselves to be in security (*amina*), whether in respect of their blood or their possessions.'[1]

Coming from [the Prophet], there is in that a demonstration of [that which constitutes] the perfection of the one whom one designates by such a noun.[2] [Just] as he said [also]:[3] 'The poor man is not the one turning about (*ṭawwāf*), who goes round people, and whom a mouthful or two, or a date or two, send away.' 'Who, then, O Messenger of God, is a poor [man]?' said [those who were listening to him]. He said: 'It is the one who does not find the wherewithal to permit him to do without others, who[se condition] is not so well known that people would bestow charity on him, and who does not ask anything of people.'[4]

Those words resemble these [other words of the Prophet]: 'Who among yourselves do you consider as one ruined (*muflis*)?' 'The one,' they said, 'who has neither dirham nor dīnār.' 'That is not the one who is ruined,' he said. 'The ruined one is rather the one who, on the Day of Resurrection, comes with good deeds as high as the mountains, yet he comes having struck such a one, insulted such another, and taken the money of such another. To that one some of his good deeds will be given, to that other other of his good

---

1 See IBN MĀJA, *Sunan*, *Fitan*, ii. 1298, no. 3934 (*ʿĀlam.* 3924); IBN ḤANBAL, *Musnad*, vi. 21, 22 (*ʿĀlam.* 22833, 22842).

2 Lit. 'whom one names by such a name'.

3 See in particular MUSLIM, *Ṣaḥīḥ*, *Zakāt*, iii. 95 (*ʿĀlam.* 1722); AL-BUKHĀRĪ, *Ṣaḥīḥ*, *Zakāt*, ii. 124–25 (*ʿĀlam.* 1382, 1385); IBN ḤANBAL, *Musnad*, ii. 316 (*ʿĀlam.* 7840).

4 Ibn Taymiyya only cites the opening words of this ḥadīth, adding 'etc.'

deeds will be given and, when no good deed of his shall remain [to his account], some of their evil deeds will be taken from them so as to be cast upon him, then he will be thrown into the Fire.'[1]

He said also: 'Who among yourselves do you consider as childless (*raqūb*[2])?' They said: 'The one who has no child.' 'The childless one,' he said, 'is the one who, in respect of his child, has nothing to present [to God].'[3]

The same goes for his words: 'The strong man (*shadīd*) is not the enraged one who wrestles [you] down (*ṣuraʿa*). The strong man is only he who remains in possession of himself, even in the event of anger.'[4]

There is something aimed at in these hadiths, namely[5] the demonstration of that which deserves, more than [the common people] think, the nouns [importing] praise or blame.

---

1 See in particular MUSLIM, *Ṣaḥīḥ*, *Birr*, viii. 18 (*ʿĀlam.* 4678); AL-TIRMIDHĪ, *Sunan*, *Ṣifat al-qiyāma*, iv. 36, no. 2533 (*ʿĀlam.* 2342); IBN ḤANBAL, *Musnad*, ii. 303, 334 (*ʿĀlam.* 8062, 8210).

2 *'raqūb'* denotes the one whose children have died before him.

3 See in particular MUSLIM, *Ṣaḥīḥ*, *Birr*, viii. 30 (*ʿĀlam.* 4722); IBN ḤANBAL, *Musnad*, i. 382–83 (*ʿĀlam.* 3445). The truly 'childless' one is, thus, not the one who, in this life, has survived his children, but the one who, in the afterlife, comes before God without any of the virtues (such as patience) that he should have demonstrated at the death of his children.

4 See in particular AL-BUKHĀRĪ, *Ṣaḥīḥ*, *Adab*, viii. 28 (*ʿĀlam.* 5649); MUSLIM, *Ṣaḥīḥ*, *Birr*, viii. 30 (*ʿĀlam.* 4723–24); IBN ḤANBAL, *Musnad*, i. 382 (*ʿĀlam.* 3444).

5 huwa + : wa

To be ruined is to be in need, and that is hateful. However, [the Messenger] has made plain that it is only on the Day of Resurrection that one will be really in need.

The lack of children, similarly, human souls think hateful on account of the want of a child who may be useful [in old age]. However, [the Messenger] has made plain that it is only in the afterlife that a child is found to be really useful, for the one who presents his children ahead of himself.[1]

In a similar way, strength and power are [things that are] desirable (*maḥbūb*). However, [the Messenger] has made plain that strength of the soul is worthier of praise than strength of the body,[2] and that it consists in remaining in possession of oneself in the event of anger. Thus, it was said to one of the Arab nobles: 'How is it that your slaves have more stamina than you in battle and in their actions?' He said: 'They have more physical stamina, whereas we have more mental stamina.'

The words of the Prophet about the noun 'Muslims' are of the [same] sort as his words about 'the Muslim', 'the believer', 'the emigrant' and 'the warrior'. [All] this conforms to what was said earlier, namely that the Legislator (*shāriʿ*) does not deny (*nafā*) [the quality] designated by a noun of Legal (*sharʿī*) import except on account of the absence (*intifāʾ*) of

---

1 That is to say, the one who submits to the judgement of the Exalted the praiseworthy comportment, patient and trusting in the divine Decision, that was his upon the decease of his children.

2 Ibn Taymiyya similarly opposes the captivity of the heart to that of the body in *Majmūʿ al-fatāwā*, trans. MICHOT, 'Textes spirituels VII', 13.

the perfection [that this noun] obligatorily demands. To flee what God has prohibited is obligatory. That Muslims should be sheltered from the enmity that a man [can make apparent] by his tongue or hand is also obligatory. In respect of their blood and their possessions, the believer (*muʾmin*) is the one before whom people feel secure (*amina*) only when he inspires [their] confidence (*amīn*); to inspire [such] confdence (*amāna*) is thus obligatory. The poor man who does not beg and who is not known has more right to be given [something] than the one who makes his need apparent and begs openly; to give him [something] is obligatory. To give to some beggar in particular rather than to another is not permitted. This being so, to give in particular to the one who does not beg is more worthy, is more obligatory and is more loved [of God].

END … AND CONTINUATION OF THE *HIJRA*

[The Prophet] said – may God pray over him and grant him peace – 'No more *hijra* after the conquest, but jihād and [good] intention [remain]! And when you are called [to jihād], go to it!'[1] He also said: 'The *hijra* shall by no means be suspended so long as the enemy remains to be fought.'[2]

1 See in particular AL-BUKHĀRĪ, *Ṣaḥīḥ*, *Ḥajj*, iii. 15 (*ʿĀlam.* 1703); MUSLIM, *Ṣaḥīḥ*, *Ḥajj*, iv. 109 (*ʿĀlam.* 2412); IBN ḤANBAL, *Musnad*, i. 226 (*ʿĀlam.* 1887). See also the study by MADELUNG of the historical context of this hadith: 'Has the Hijra come to an end?', 225–26.

2 See in particular AL-NASĀʾĪ, *Sunan*, *Bayʿa*, vii. 146 (*ʿĀlam.* 4102); IBN ḤANBAL, *Musnad*, i. 192 (*ʿĀlam.* 1581); see also MADELUNG, 'Has the Hijra come to an end?', 227–28, 235.

Each of these two [statements] is true.

By the first, [the Prophet] meant the *hijra* to which people were used in his time, namely the *hijra* toward Madina, departing from Makka or some other [regions] of the land of the Arabs. This *hijra* was prescribed by the Law (*mashrūʿ*) when Makka and some other regions were a domain of unbelief and war (*dār kufr wa-ḥarb*) and the faith was in Madina. Emigration from the domain of unbelief toward the domain of Islam was obligatory upon whoever had the means to do it.[1] When Makka was conquered and became a

---

1 'The Emigrants (*muhājir*) emigrated from Makka and some other [regions] toward Madina. A group among them, such as ʿUmar, ʿUthmān and Jaʿfar b. Abī Ṭālib, even emigrated twice: they emigrated to Abyssinia and they emigrated to Madina. Islam, at that time, was little [in strength] while the unbelievers dominated the whole of the earth. In Makka, [the Muslims] were persecuted and suffered, from their near [kin] and others among the associators (*mushrik*), such persecutions as none [really] knows except God. They were [however] steadfast under persecution and drank the bitterness of affliction, quit their homes and departed from their friends for the love of God and His Messenger, so waging the jihād on His path. Thus God, Exalted is He, has described them in saying: "… [and it is] for the poor emigrants who have been expelled from their houses and their possessions, seeking a favour from God and [His] pleasure, and they are helping God and His Messenger. Those are the truthful" [Qurʾān, *al-Ḥashr*, 59. 8]. They did all this willingly and from choice, of their own volition. Nothing forced them to do it, no one constrained them to it. By way of force, Islam at that time had nothing that could have compelled anyone to become Muslim. The Prophet, may God pray over him and grant him peace, and those who followed him were, at that time, forbidden to fight and com-

domain of Islam, with the Arabs entering into Islam, this land [of Arabia] as a whole became a domain of Islam. The Prophet therefore said: 'No more *hijra* after the conquest…'.

Whether a land is a domain of unbelief or a domain of faith or of perverts is not an attribute that is a necessary concomitant (*lāzim*). It is, rather, an accidental attribute, correlative to its inhabitants. Every land whose inhabitants are the

---

manded to withdraw and be patient. Nobody became Muslim except* by choice. Nobody emigrated except by choice.
'That is why Aḥmad b. Ḥanbal and some other ulema said that there was no hypocrite among the Emigrants, and that hypocrisy only emerged within the tribes of the Helpers (*anṣār*), when Islam appeared in Madina and the tribes of Aws and Khazraj entered into [Islam]. When the Muslims came to have a domain out of which to defend themselves, and [when they came] to fight, there were, among the inhabitants of Madina and the Bedouin (*aʿrāb*) of the surrounding territory who entered into Islam, some who entered into it from dread or fear, being hypocrites as the Exalted has said: "Among the Bedouin who surround you are some hypocrites, and among the inhabitants of Madina. They are obstinate in their hypocrisy. You do not know them, but We know them. We shall double their torment" [Qurʾān, *al-Tawba*, 9. 101]. And that is why it is only in the Madinan sūras that hypocrisy is mentioned. As for the Makkan sūras, there is no mention of hypocrites in them. Those who had become Muslim in Makka before the *Hijra*, there was no hypocrite among them. Those who emigrated, there was no hypocrite among them. They were, on the contrary, people who believed in God and in His Messenger, loved God and His Messenger, and by whom God and His Messenger were better loved than their children or their kin or their possessions." (IBN TAYMIYYA, *Minhāj al-sunnat al-nabawiyya* (1989), vii. 475–76.) * illā + : aḥad **M**

believers, who fear [God], is, at that moment, a domain of the Friends of God. Every land whose inhabitants are the unbelievers is, at that moment, a domain of unbelief. Every land whose inhabitants are the perverts is, at that moment, a domain of perversity. If others than those we have mentioned [come to] dwell in a [land], and if it is transformed by those others, it is their domain.

The same holds for the mosque: when it is transformed into a tavern or becomes a house of perversity, a house of injustice, or a church in which associates are given to God, its [status] is correlative to [the condition of] its occupants. The same holds for the house of wine, or of perversity, etc.: if it is made into a mosque in which God, the Majestic and Mighty, is worshipped, its [status] is correlative to that [condition]. Thus again the virtuous man may become a perverted one, the unbeliever may become a believer, or the believer may become an unbeliever, etc.: [the status] of each is correlative to the transition of [his] conditions (*ḥāl*) from one condition to another.

God, Exalted is He, has said:[1] 'God offers you as a similitude a township: it was in security, calm, its provisions reaching it in abundance from everywhere, and it denied the bounties of God and God made it taste the violence of hunger and fear, on account of what they had done.' This [verse] was sent down about Makka, when it was a domain of unbelief, but which, in itself, had not ceased to be the

---

1 Qur'ān, *al-Naḥl*, 16. 112. In fact Ibn Taymiyya cites only the opening words, indicating the rest by: 'and the verse'.

best land of God, and the [one] most loved of [the Prophet]: He had only meant to speak of its inhabitants.

Al-Tirmidhī has reported, in a tradition going back to the Prophet (*marfūʿ*) that he said to Makka, while standing in the

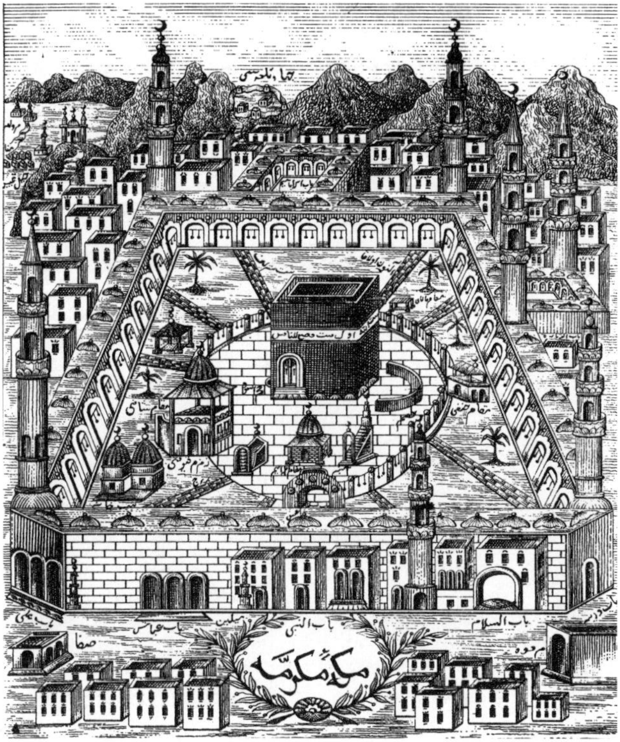

Makka[1]

1 Detail of a lithograph from an Uzbek translation of *Dalāʾil al-khayrāt* by Muḥammad al-Jazūlī (d. *c.* 869/1465), (St. Petersburg/Tashkent, 1312/1894), 59.

Ḥazwara:[1] 'By God! You are truly the best land of God, and the land of God most beloved of God. But for the fact that my people forced me to depart from you, I would not have left.'[2] In a[nother] narration: 'the best land of God and the land of God most loved by me.'[3]

It is plain therefore that Makka is the land most beloved of God and His Messenger. [Nevertheless,] to him and those of the believers who were with him, staying in Madina was better than staying in Makka, given that it was the place of their *hijra.*

It is for that [reason] that standing guard (*ribāṭ*) in the frontier strongholds[4] (*thaghr*) is better than settling (*mujāwara*)

---

1 'Marketplace of Makka, which was adjoined to the mosque when it was expanded.' (YĀQŪT, *Muʿjam al-buldān*, ii. 294)

2 See AL-TIRMIDHĪ, *Sunan*, *Manāqib*, v. 380, no. 4017 (*ʿĀlam.* 3860); AL-DĀRIMĪ, *Sunan*, *Siyar*, ii. 239 (*ʿĀlam.* 2398); IBN ḤANBAL, *Musnad*, iv. 305 (*ʿĀlam.* 17966).

3 See IBN MĀJA, *Sunan*, *Manāsik*, ii. 1037, no. 3108 (*ʿĀlam.* 3099).

4 As [examples] of 'the Muslims' [frontier] strongholds' where some [Muslims] would present themselves in order to 'stand guard' (*ribāṭ*), it comes to Ibn Taymiyya to mention 'the strongholds of Syria (*al-Shām*) such as Ashkalon, Acre, Tortosa, Mount Lebanon, etc., the strongholds of Egypt such as Alexandria, etc., the strongholds of Iraq such as Abadan, etc.' (IBN TAYMIYYA, *Qāʿida fī ziyāra Bayt al-Maqdis*, 15)

'A stronghold may be a [particular] place. The Muslims subsequently conquer the regions adjacent to them and the stronghold [then] comes to be transferred to the [new] frontiers of their territory. That is why a place sometimes is a stronghold and sometimes is not. Just as [a place] is sometimes a domain of Islam and of piety, sometimes a domain of unbelief and perversity. In just the same way Makka also was a domain of unbelief and war, while Madina was a domain of faith, of emigration (*hijra*), and a place for standing guard. When Makka was conquered, it became a domain of Islam and Madina remained no longer a place of emigration (*hijra*) and standing guard as it had been before the conquest of Makka. Rather, [the Prophet], may God pray over him and grant him peace, said: "No more *hijra* after the conquest, but jihād and [good] intention [remain]. And when you are called [to jihād], go to it!" [As of then] the strongholds became the confines of the land of the Hijaz adjacent to the land of war: the land of Syria and the land of Iraq. Thereafter, when the Muslims conquered Syria and Iraq, the strongholds became, in Syria, the [Mediterranean] sea coasts such as Ashkalon, Acre, and the neighbouring regions; in Iraq, Abadan, etc. It is for that [reason] that there is much mention of Ashkalon and Abadan in the arguments of writers in the earlier times [of Islam]: both were [frontier] strongholds. Tortosa also was a stronghold while it belonged to the Muslims. When the unbelievers captured it, the stronghold became the region of the country of Aleppo, adjacent to the enemy's territory.' (Ibn Taymiyya, *Majmūᶜ al-fatāwā*, xxvii. 248–49)

'The virtuous among the believers would stand guard in the strongholds. Thus al-Awzāᶜī, Abū Isḥāq al-Fazārī, Makhlad b. al-Ḥusayn, Ibrāhīm b. Adham, ᶜAbd Allāh b. al-Mubārak, Ḥudhayfat al-Marᶜashī, Yūsuf b. Asbāṭ and some others stood guard in the Syrian strongholds. Among them were some who came from Khurāsān, Iraq, and other places, to stand guard in the Syrian strongholds.

'It was indeed the inhabitants of Syria who fought the Nazarenes, the People of the Book. Now, in the *Sunan*, [it is reported] of the Prophet, may God pray over him and grant him peace, that he said: "The one slain by the People of the Book, his is the reward of two martyrs!" (See ABŪ DĀʾŪD, *al-Sunan*, *Jihād*, iii. 5–6, no. 2488 (*ᶜĀlam*. 2129).) That [is so] because these [People of the Book] fight for religion (*ᶜalā dīn*). As for the unbelieving Turks and their like, they do not fight for religion.

in Makka or Madina. Thus it is established in the *Ṣaḥīḥ* [that the Prophet said]: 'Standing guard (*ribāṭ*) for a day and a night on the path of God is better than fasting a month and spending it in vigil. Whoever dies while standing guard (*murābiṭ*) dies as a warrior (*mujāhid*). His [meritorious] deed follows after him [until the Day of Resurrection], his provisions come to him from the Garden in abundance, and he is protected from the torment of the grave."[1] In the *Sunan* [it is also reported] from ʿUthmān that the Prophet, may God pray over him and grant him peace, said: "Standing guard for one day on the path of God is better than to settle down for a

When those [People of the Book] are victorious, they therefore ravage (*afsada*) the religion and the sovereign power (*mulk*). As for the Turks, they ravage the sovereign power and whatever of the religion follows that [power]; they do not fight for religion.

'That is why there are numerous mentions of Tortosa in the books on [religious] knowledge (*ʿilm*) and jurisprudence (*fiqh*) composed at the time: it was *the* stronghold of the Muslims – so much so indeed that Aḥmad b. Ḥanbal, al-Sarī al-Saqaṭī and other ulema and shaykhs also presented themselves there, in order to stand guard. And [the caliph] al-Maʾmūn died in its environs.' (IBN TAYMIYYA, *Majmūʿ al-fatāwā*, xxvii. 52–53)

On the exhortation, under the Umayyads, to emigrate to Syria, see also MADELUNG, 'Has the Hijra come to an end?', 226–28, 233–34.

1 See in particular MUSLIM, *Ṣaḥīḥ*, *Imāra*, vi. 52 (*ʿĀlam.* 3537); IBN MĀJA, *Sunan*, *Jihād*, ii. 924, no. 2767 (*ʿĀlam.* 2757); IBN ḤANBAL, *Musnad*, v. 440 (*ʿĀlam.* 22611). Also cited by IBN TAYMIYYA in *Qāʿida fī ziyāra Bayt al-Maqdis*, 15.

thousand days elsewhere."[1] And Abū Hurayra[2] said: "Assuredly I would rather stand guard for a night on the path of God than stand [in vigil] on the Night of Power (*laylat al-qadr*) next to the Black Stone!"[3]

---

1 See AL-TIRMIDHĪ, *Sunan*, *Faḍāʾil al-jihād*, iii. 108, no. 1718 (*ʿĀlam.* 1590); al-NASĀʾĪ, *Sunan*, *Jihād*, vi. 40 (*ʿĀlam.* 3118); IBN ḤANBAL, *Musnad*, i. 65 (*ʿĀlam.* 440).

2 Companion (d. *c.* 58/678); see J. Robson, *EI*[2] art. 'Abū Hurayrah'.

3 'Standing guard (*ribāṭ*) in the strongholds, the ulema have said, is better than to settle (*mujāwara*) in the neighbourhood of the two noble sanctuaries [Makka and Madina]. Standing guard (*murābaṭa*) is connected to the genus (*jins*) of jihād, whereas settling down [in Makka, etc.] is connected to the genus of pilgrimage (*ḥajj*). Now the genus of jihād is higher – there is unanimous accord of the Muslims on that – than the genus of pilgrimage. Thus the Exalted said: "Do you liken giving drink to the pilgrims and maintaining the Inviolable Mosque to [the deed of] one who believes in God and the Last Day and fights (*jāhada*) on the path of God? For God the two are not equal, and God does not guide the wrongdoing people. Those who have believed, emigrated (*hājara*) and fought on the path of God with their possessions and their persons occupy in the sight of God a greater degree, and those are the winners" [Qurʾān, *al-Tawba*, 9. 19–20]. (IBN TAYMIYYA, *Majmūʿ al-fatāwā*, xxvii. 142–43; see also, p.52.)

'Standing guard (*murābaṭa*) on the path of God is better than settling (*mujāwara*) in Makka, Madina and Jerusalem. Abū Hurayra, may God be pleased with him, even said: "Assuredly, I would rather stand guard for a night on the path of God than spend the Night of Power (*laylat al-qadr*) next to the Black Stone." He would prefer to stand guard for a night than worship [God] during the most eminent of nights in the most eminent of [all] places. It is also for that [reason] that the

That is why the best land, for what is of merit for any man, is a land where he is more obedient to God and His Messenger. This varies as situations (*ḥāl*) vary, and by no means is the land identified where it would be better for one to settle. The best, for what is of merit for any man, is correlative only to fear [of God] and to obedience, to humility, to submission [to God's will], and to attentiveness.

Abū l-Dardāʾ[1] wrote to Salmān:[2] 'Come to the Holy Land!'[3] Salmān wrote to him: 'A land does not make anyone holy. It is only his action that makes a servant holy!' The Prophet, may God pray over him and grant him peace, had established the tie of brotherhood between Salmān and Abū

Prophet, may God pray over him and grant him peace, and his Companions resided in Madina rather than in Makka. Among the reasons [for doing so] there was [the reason] that, in Madina, they were standing guard (*murābiṭ*).' (IBN TAYMIYYA, *Majmūʿ al-fatāwā*, xxviii. 418. See also: *ibid.*, 5–6, 12; *Qāʿida fī ziyāra Bayt al-Maqdis*, 15.)

1 Abū l-Dardāʾ al-Anṣārī l-Khazrajī (d. 32/652), Companion; see A. Jeffery, *EI*[2] art. 'Abū l-Dardāʾ'.

2 Salmān al-Fārisī, famous Companion of Persian origin (d. 35/655 or 36/656?); see G. Levi della Vida, *EI*[2] art. 'Salmān al-Fārisī'.

3 See Qurʾān, *al-Māʾida*, 5. 21: 'O my people! Enter into the Holy Land that God has assigned for you.' It is quite certain that Abū l-Dardāʾ meant *al-arḍ al-muqaddasa*, with the passive participle, as in the Qurʾān, 'the Land sanctified'. Salmān surely exploited the fact that Abū l-Dardāʾ did not mark vowels in his message to make a play on the words and to read the participle as active, *al-arḍ al-muqaddisa*, 'the Land sanctifying' – whence his answer.

l-Dardāʾ. Salmān was more learned than Abū l-Dardāʾ in [diverse] things, notably this one.

God, Exalted is He, said to Moses, upon him be peace: 'I will show you the land of the perverted' [Qurʾān, *al-Aʿrāf*, 7. 145], namely the domain where the Amalikites[1] were, and which subsequently became the domain of the believers. It refers to the domain that the Qurʾān has indicated as being the Holy Land and the land of Egypt, of which God made the sons of Israel the inheritors.

Jerusalem[2]

---

1 People of the borderlands of the Idumea, mentioned in the Bible (Isaiah, 34. 6), whose moral corruption is emphasized in the Muslim literary tradition, and who were eradicated by David. See G. Vajda, EI^2 art. ' ʿAmālīḳ'.

2 Detail of a xylograph from VON BREYDENBACH, *Peregrinatio in Terram Sanctam* (1498).

The situations (*ḥāl*) of countries are thus like the situations of the servants:[1] a man is at one time a Muslim, at

---

1 'The statuses of regions change by virtue of the change in the situations of their inhabitants. A region may be a domain of unbelief when its inhabitants are unbelievers. It then becomes a domain of Islam when its inhabitants become Muslims. Thus Makka, may God ennoble it, was to begin with a domain of unbelief and of war, and God said about it: "How many cities, much stronger than your city, which has expelled you, [have We caused to perish]!" [Qurʾān, *Muḥammad*, 47. 13]. Then, when the Prophet, may God pray over him and grant him peace, conquered it, it became a domain of Islam. And it is, in itself, the Mother of cities and the land most beloved of God.
'Similarly for the Holy Land where were found the giants that God, Exalted is He, has mentioned. Thus the Exalted said: "When Moses said to his people: 'O my people, remember the grace that God heaped upon you when He placed prophets among you, and He made you kings, and gave to you something that He had given to no one in the worlds! O my people, enter into the Holy Land that God has assigned for you and do not turn backwards: you would turn on your backs as losers!' They said: 'O Moses, there are a giant people therein, and we will not enter therein until they have gone out of it. If they go out of it, we will enter…' " and the verses [that follow; Qurʾān, *al-Māʾida*, 5. 20–22]. The Exalted also said, when he saved Moses and his people from the drowning: 'I will cause you to see the domain of the perverted' [Qurʾān, *al-Aʿrāf*, 7. 145]. These were domains of the perverted when, at that time, the perverted inhabited them. Subsequently, when the virtuous inhabited them, they became the domain of the virtuous.
'This is a fundamental that it is necessary to be aware of: a land may be praised or blamed at certain moments on account of the situation of its inhabitants; subsequently, the situation of its inhabitants changes and the judgement [to make] about them changes accordingly. Praise and blame, reward and pun-

another an unbeliever, at one time a believer and at another a hypocrite, at one time pious and fearful [of God], at another perverted, and at [yet] another depraved and wretched. Thus places of habitation are correlative to their inhabitants.[1] And

---

ishment indeed follow only from faith and virtuous action, or the contrary thereof – unbelief, perversity and disobedience. God, Exalted is He, has said: "O mankind! Fear your Lord Who created you from a single soul, created from that [soul] its mate, and from the pair of them, He made spread [over the earth] many men and women. Fear God, through Whom you ask [things] of one another, and [maintain] the ties of blood' [Qurʾān, *al-Nisāʾ*, 4. 1]. And the Prophet – may God pray over him and grant him peace – said: "An Arab is not pre-eminent over a non-Arab, nor a non-Arab over an Arab, nor a white over a black, nor a black over a white, except through [their] fear [of God]." [See IBN ḤANBAL, *Musnad*, v. 411 (*ʿĀlam.* 22391).] "Mankind are the sons of Adam and Adam [was created] from dust." [See in particular AL-TIRMIDHĪ, *Sunan*, *Tafsīr*, v. 65, no. 3324 (*ʿĀlam.* 3193); IBN ḤANBAL, *Musnad*, ii. 361 (*ʿĀlam.* 8381).] When he established a bond of brotherhood between the Emigrants and the Helpers, the Prophet, may God pray over him and grant him peace, established one between Abū l-Dardāʾ and Salmān the Persian. While Abū l-Dardāʾ was in Syria and Salmān in Iraq, as deputy for ʿUmar b. al-Khaṭṭāb, he wrote to him: "Come to the Holy Land!" Salmān wrote to him: "A land does not make anyone holy. It is only his action that makes a man holy!" ' (IBN TAYMIYYA, *Majmūʿ al-fatāwā*, xxvii. 143–44)

1 'Makka, may God protect it, is of all places the noblest. During the exile (*ghurba*) of Islam it was [nevertheless] a domain of unbelief and of war where it was forbidden to reside. After the *Hijra* also, it was forbidden to the Emigrants to go back there to reside.

for a man to emigrate (*hijra*) from a place of unbelief and disobedience to a place of faith and obedience is like his

---

'In the time of Moses, upon him be peace, before he departed from [Egypt] with the children of Israel, Syria was the domain of the Ṣabean associators, of the perverted giants. And the Exalted, referring to it, said to the children of Israel: "I will cause you to see the domain of the perverted" [Qur'ān, *al-Aʿrāf*, 7. 145].

'The fact that a land is a domain of unbelief or a domain of Islam or of faith, a domain of peace or of war, a domain of obedience or of disobedience, a domain of the believers or of the perverted – these are accidental qualities, not necessary concomitants. [A land] thus passes from one quality to another, just as a man, in his soul, passes from unbelief to faith and knowledge, and vice versa. As for nobility that is enduring in all times and [in all] places, it [is found] in faith and virtuous action.' (IBN TAYMIYYA, *Majmūʿ al-fatāwā*, xxvii. 45)

'What one generally finds in the arguments [of authors] of the past about the eminence of Ashkalon, or of Alexandria, of Acre, of Qazwīn, or of yet other [places] – what one finds [on that] by way of narrations about the virtuous [people] who [lived] in such places, etc., is owed to the fact that these were strongholds, not to [some intrinsic] property that such a place might have. Now, that a place is for the Muslims a stronghold or something else is among the attributes [which] for [this place are] accidental, not necessary concomitants – in the same way as the fact of [its] being domain of Islam or domain of unbelief, domain of war or domain of peace, domain of knowledge and faith or domain of ignorance and hypocrisy. This indeed differs according to the difference of the inhabitants [of the place] and their attributes – in contrast to the three mosques [of Makka, Madina, and Jerusalem]. What distinguishes these [mosques] is indeed, in them, an attribute necessarily concomitant – it is not possible to strip them of it.' (IBN TAYMIYYA, *Majmūʿ al-fatāwā*, xxvii. 53–54)

repenting and passing from unbelief and disobedience to faith and obedience: it is a command that will remain [in force] until the Day of Resurrection.

God, Exalted is He, has said: 'Those who afterwards believed and emigrated from their homes and fought with you, those are of you' [Qurʾān, *al-Anfāl*, 8. 75]. In this [category], said a group of the Ancients (*salaf*), is included whoever believes, emigrates (*hājara*) and fights, until the Day of Resurrection. So also [for these] words of God, Exalted is He: 'As for those who emigrated (*hājara*) after they had been tested, then fought and were steadfast, assuredly your Lord, after such things, is indeed forgiving, merciful' [Qurʾān, *al-Naḥl*, 16. 110]. What is signified by these [words] concerns every individual whom Satan has tested [in order to distance him] from his religion or whom he causes to fall into disobedience, who then flees from (*hajara*) evil deeds, fights against himself and other enemies, fights against the hypocrites by bidding to the good and forbidding from the reprehensible, etc., and who is patient and persevering in the face of whatever strikes him – [of] word or deed.

And God, the All-praised and Exalted, knows better!

III. A DOUBLE REALITY

[Ibn Taymiyya] – may God have mercy on him – also said:

As for the one who abandons the prayer and his likes – those who publicly let themselves go in innovation or some perversity – well, the judgement of a Muslim will be of diverse kinds as was [the judgement] of God's Messenger, may God pray over him and grant him peace, in respect of

Makka and Madina. The judgement of the one who is capable of inflicting a penalty on these [people] by turning away [fleeing from them] is not at all the judgement of one who is not [so] capable, and turning away from some people with whom one has no need to keep company is not like turning away from those with whom one has [such] need.

The fundamental [to take account of] is that turning away (*hijra*) from perverts is [a reality] of two kinds: turning away as [sheer] quitting (*hijra tark*) and turning away in order to inflict a penalty (*hijra taᶜzīr*).[1]

The first [kind of turning away] is indicated in these words of the Exalted [Qurʾān, *al-Muzzammil*, 73. 10]: 'Turn away from them in a comely manner!' Also by these [Qurʾān, *al-Nisāʾ*, 4. 140]: 'This has been revealed to you in the Book: when you hear the verses of God denied and derided, do not remain seated with these people until they engage themselves in some other subject.' Also related to this type [of turning away] is the emigration (*hijra*) of a Muslim quitting the domain of war (*dār al-ḥarb*). What is aimed at by that is that the Muslim turn away from evil deeds and turn away from the servants of evil whose company is harmful to him, unless to serve a preponderant need or interest (*maṣlaḥa*) [to stay with them].

---

1 'What is aimed at by *hijra* is one of the two [following] things: either quitting (*tark*) the faults to be escaped (*mahjūr*) and their authors, or chastising the one who commits them and punishing him for deterrence (*nikāl*).' (IBN TAYMIYYA, *Majmūᶜ al-fatāwā*, x. 377)

The burial place and mosque of the Prophet in Madina[1]

As for turning away in order to inflict a penalty, [one will do so] as the Prophet, may God pray over him and grant him peace, and his Companions turned away from 'the three

---

1 Detail of a lithograph from an Uzbek translation of *Dalāʾil al-Khayrāt* by Muḥammad al-Jazūlī (St. Petersburg/Tashkent, 1312/1894), 59.

who were left behind',[1] and as ʿUmar and the Muslims turned away from Ṣabīgh.[2] [Turning away from someone] in

---

1 See the Qurʾān, *al-Tawba*, 9. 118: 'God accepts also the repentance of the three who were left behind…' On the occasion of the summer expedition in 9/630 against Tabūk, the poet Kaʿb b. Mālik and two other Muslims delayed their departure under false pretexts. The Prophet punished them by forbidding all contact with them. The revelation of this verse later re-integrated them to the community.
'The Prophet, may God pray over him and grant him peace, commanded turning away (*hajr*) from "the three who had been left behind" for fifty nights. Subsequently, God accepted their repentance and the Muslims [again] conversed with them.' (IBN TAYMIYYA, *Minhāj al-sunnat al-nabawiyya fī naqḍ kalām al-Shīʿat al-qadariyya* [1989], vi. 354)
'It has been averred about the Prophet that he said: "For a Muslim, it is not lawful to turn away from his brother more than three [occasions], the one turning his back on the other when they meet. The better of the two is the one who resumes greeting [the other by wishing him peace]" [see AL-BUKHĀRĪ, *Ṣaḥīḥ*, *Istiʾdhān*, viii. 53 (*ʿĀlam.* 5768); MUSLIM, *Ṣaḥīḥ*, *Birr*, viii. 9 (*ʿĀlam.* 4643)]. Yes, it has been averred about him that he turned away from Kaʿb b. Mālik and his two companions, may God be pleased with them, when, on the occasion of the Tabūk expedition, they remained behind, so that their disobedience was a public matter and it was feared that they were hypocrites. [The Prophet] turned away from them and ordered the Muslims to turn away from them. He even ordered [the three] to stay apart from, without repudiating, their wives, for fifty nights, until the moment when the acceptance of their repentance came down from Heaven.' (IBN TAYMIYYA, *Majmūʿ al-fatāwā*, xxiv. 174)

2 ' ʿUmar – may God be pleased with him – similarly ordered the Muslims to turn away from Ṣabīgh b. ʿIsl al-Tamīmī when he saw him [as being] among those who used to put [undue]

emphasis on that which, in the Book, is ambivalent. [That continued] until a year had passed and the sincerity of his repentance had become evident. [ʿUmar then] ordered the Muslims to reunite with him.

'From this and similar cases, Muslims have counselled turning away from those in whom the marks of deviancy are publicly apparent – those who publicly adopt innovations, invite others to [adopt] them, and those who publicly [commit] major sins. As for one who keeps a disobedience hidden or keeps secret some inexpiable innovation – he is not turned away from. Only he who invites [others to adopt] an innovation is turned away from. Turning away [from someone] is indeed a kind of punishment and one does not punish except one who publicly [commits] a disobedience in word or deed. Someone who publicly [wishes] us well, we accept what he makes show of (*ʿalāniya*) [towards us], and we entrust to God, Exalted is He, [the responsibility of judging] his secret thought (*sarīra*). He may be, at most, equivalent to the hypocrites from whom the Prophet, may God pray over him and grant him peace, accepted what they made show of [towards him] and entrusted to God the [responsibility of] judging their secret thoughts when they came to him, in the year of Tabūk, swearing oaths and putting forward their excuses. It is for that [reason] that Imām Aḥmad b. Ḥanbal, and the majority of the imāms before him and after him such as Mālik [b. Anas] and others, do not accept the narration (*riwāya*) [of ḥadīths] from one who invites [others to adopt] an innovation, and they do not keep company with him, as distinct from [what they do with an innovator] who holds his silence. The authors of the *Ṣaḥīḥ*s have collected [ḥadīths] from groups of people accused of innovation who held their silence but have not collected [any] from those who invited [others to adopt] innovations.' (IBN TAYMIYYA, *Majmūʿ al-fatāwā*, xxiv. 174–75; the sequel of the second passage quoted in the preceding note.)

' ʿUmar – may God be pleased with him – put a ban on (*nafā*) Ṣabīgh b. ʿIsl al-Tamīmī when he publicly emphasized the ambivalent [verses of the Qurʾān] "seeking discord therein and looking for an interpretation thereof" [Qurʾān, *Āl ʿImrān*, 3. 7]. He struck him and commanded the Muslims to turn away from him for a year [even] after he had publicly shown his repentance. When he repented [for a year, ʿUmar] commanded the Muslims to converse with him [again].

'Inspired by that, Aḥmad [b. Ḥanbal] and others deferred a year [before reintegration into the community] for the one who invites to innovation when he repents. Just as ʿUmar had deferred [the reintegration of] Ṣabīgh. Similarly for the perverted one when he repents and one takes into consideration, in addition to [his] repentance, the virtuous character of [his] action – just as al-Shāfiʿī and Aḥmad [b. Ḥanbal] say, according to one of the two versions [of his juristic positions].' (IBN TAYMIYYA, *Minhāj al-sunnat al-nabawiyya*, vi. 354–55)

' ʿUmar struck Ṣabīgh b. ʿIsl because [Ṣabīgh's] objective, in asking some questions about the ambivalent [verses of the Qurʾān], was to seek out dissension. He [was asking them] in the manner of one who submits some questions and raises some problems in connection with the arguments of another, [in the manner of one] who says: "What did he mean by that?", and whose goal is to incite doubt and to attack him, not to get to know the truth.' (IBN TAYMIYYA, *Majmūʿ al-fatāwā*, xvii. 394)

'When Ṣabīgh b. ʿIsl al-Tamīmī came to ʿUmar b. al-Khaṭṭāb, may God be pleased with him, [and] asked him the questions that he asked him about the ambivalent [verses of the Qurʾān] "seeking discord therein and looking for an interpretation thereof", and ʿUmar struck him roughly, he uncovered his head and noticed that he had two plaits. He said to him: "If I had found you [with your skull] shaved, I would have struck you there where your two eyes are." In fact, if he had found him [with his skull] shaved, he would have had an indication thereby that he was among the Khārijīs, going out [of Islam] – he used to kill them on account of the command to fight against them [given] by the Prophet, may God pray over him

this way is a kind of chastisement.[1] When, by the fact of thus turning away from someone, the outcome is that one obtains something good and desirable (*maʿrūf*), and pushes away something that is reprehensible (*munkar*), [doing so] is prescribed by the Law (*mashrūʿ*). When [on the contrary] the outcome thereof is a corruption still greater than that from the fault [that one was thinking to chastise], doing so is not prescribed by the Law. And God knows better![2]

---

and grant him peace.' (IBN TAYMIYYA, *al-Istiqāma* [2000], i. 258)

1 'The complete *hijra* is turning away (*hijra*) from bad deeds and their practitioners. Thus it is a fleeing (*hijrān*) from those who invite to innovations, fleeing from the perverted and fleeing from whoever mixes himself in with all of those or gives them assistance. The same [goes] also for whoever abandons the fight (*jihād*), without which there is nothing of general good (*maṣlaḥa*) for [the people]: he will be chastised in their turning away from him for not having helped them in piety and fear [of God]. Adulterers, homosexuals, the one who abandons the fight (*jihād*), the practitioners of innovations and the drinkers of wine – all these people and those who mix in with them are a harm for the religion of Islam. There is no help [to be found] among them, neither in piety nor in fear [of God]. One who does not turn away from them is abandoning that which is commanded and doing that which is forbidden.' (IBN TAYMIYYA, *Majmūʿ al-fatāwā*, xv. 311–12)

2 *Ibid.*, xxviii. 216–17.

IV. APPROPRIATE SEVERITY

[Ibn Taymiyya] – may God have mercy on him – also said:

SECTION ON THE QUESTIONS OF ISḤĀQ B. MANṢŪR[1]

In the *Book of the Sunna*, chapter 'On the action of avoiding (*mujānaba*) one who says: "The Qurʾān is created" ', al-Khallāl[2] says of Isḥāq that he said to Abū ʿAbd Allāh[3] [b. Ḥanbal]:

Someone who said: 'The Qur'an is created' …

'… May he be struck by every calamity!'

'Shall we show them enmity or shall we put up with them?'

'The people of Khurāsān will not be of [sufficient] force to fight against them.'

This answer of Ibn Ḥanbal [should be considered in relation] to his words about the partisans of [the doctrine of]

---

1 Isḥāq b. Manṣūr b. Bahrām Abū Yaʿqūb al-Kawsaj al-Marwazī (d. 251/865), disciple of Ibn Ḥanbal. See IBN ABĪ YAʿLĀ, *Ṭabaqāt al-Ḥanābila* [1997], i. 106–08.

2 Aḥmad AL-KHALLĀL (d. 311/923), author of the first grand corpus of Ḥanbalī law. See H. Laoust, *EI*[2] art. 'al-Khallāl'. The citation comes from his *Sunna*, vol. 7 – the volume not edited by al-Zahrānī – see the London MS, *BL Or. 2675*, fol. 189[r] (Ar. 186), ll. 17–20.

3 ʿAbd Allāh (d. 290/903), son of Ibn Ḥanbal, who transmitted the major part of his works. See H. Laoust, *EI*[2] art. 'Aḥmad b. Ḥanbal'.

the power [of man over his acts] (*qadariyya*):[1] 'If we cease to report [some ḥadīths] from the Qadarīs, we will cease to report them from the greater part of the people of Baṣra!' [It should also be considered in relation] to the way in which he acted with them during the 'Inquisition' (*miḥna*),[2] whether this consisted in rebuffing them 'in the best manner'[3] or addressing to them some arguments. [All of that] elucidates what [one finds] in his arguments and his actions, in respect of turning away [from these people] and prohibiting keeping company and conversing with them – he even turned away, in other circumstances, from [certain] well-known [individuals] among the great personages, and commanded turning away from them on account of a sort of 'jahmization'[4] on their part.

TO FLEE AND TO CHASTISE

Fleeing (*hijra*) [someone] is one sort of penalty (*taᶜzīr*) among others, and to chastise is one of the sorts of the emigration (*hijra*) that consists in abandoning bad deeds.

---

1 The partisans of *qadar* in the sense of 'capacity' (*qudra*), of man's 'power' over his actions, that is to say, free will. See J. Van Ess, *EI²* art. 'Ḳadariyya'.

2 The period (213–34/833–48) in which the ᶜAbbāsid caliph al-Maᵓmūn and his two successors imposed by force the dogma of the creation of the Qurᵓān. See M. Hinds, *EI²* art. 'Miḥna'.

3 See Qurᵓān, *al-Naḥl*, 16. 125: 'And dispute with them in the best manner.'

4 *al-tajahhum*, meaning the adoption of the theological ideas of Abū Mūḥriz Jahm b. Ṣafwān (d. 128/746). See W. M. Watt, *EI²* art. 'D̲jahm b. Ṣafwān' and 'D̲jahmiyya'; MICHOT, 'Textes spirituels VI', 15; 'XV', 26–27; 'XVI', 24.

The Prophet said – may God pray over him and grant him peace: 'The emigrant (*muhājir*) is one who flees bad deeds.'[1] He also said: '…someone who flees what God has prohibited.'[2] That is a fleeing for fear [of God] (*hijrat al-taqwā*).

For that which is a fleeing [that entails] a penalty and a jihād, one has the example [of the Prophet] turning away from 'the three who had been left behind' and commanding the Muslims to turn away from them, until their repentance was accepted.

At times therefore, turning away (*hijra*) is connected to the genus of fear [of God], when it is do with turning away from bad deeds, as the Exalted has said [Qurʾān, *al-Anʿām*, 6. 68–69]: 'And when you see them engaging in disputation of Our verses, turn yourself from them until they engage in another matter. And if Satan causes you to forget, no longer remain, after you remember, sitting with the unjust people. Those who fear [God] are not burdened with any obligation to bring them to a reckoning but to address to them a reminder. It may be that they will fear [God]!' He has thus made it plain – Praised is He – that the ones fearful [of God] are the opposite of the unjust ones, and that those who have the command to quit (*hijrān*) the gatherings, in the course of which people engage in disputation of the verses of God, are the ones fearful [of God].

At other times also turning away (*hijra*) belongs to the genus of jihād, to bidding to the good and the desitable and

---

1 See in particular IBN ḤANBAL, *Musnad*, ii. 215 (*ʿĀlam.* 6721).

2 See above, p. 67.

forbidding from the reprehensible, to implementing the sanctions, and it consists of chastising the one who transgresses and is unjust.

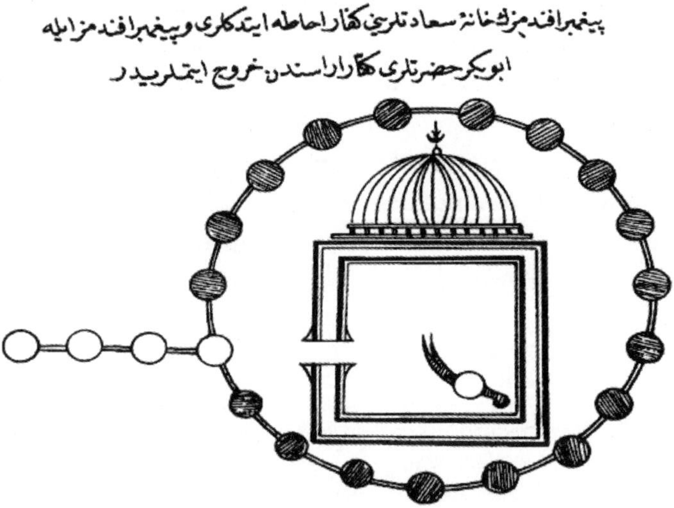

The Prophet (with Abū Bakr) leaving his house, encircled by the unbelievers[1]

Chastising the unjust one and inflicting upon him a penalty are conditional upon being capable [of doing so]. That is why, in respect of the two kinds of turning away (*hijra*), the judgement of the Law differentiates between the one who is capable [of doing it] and the one who is not; and likewise

---

1 Lithographic illustration from YĀZĪJĪ ZĀDEH, *Kitāb al-Muḥammadiyya fī l-kamālāt al-Aḥmadiyya* (1867), 124.

between a restricted number [of individuals] of the type of unjust innovator and an abundance of them, between their strength and their weakness. Similarly, the judgement [of the Law] differentiates in the same way for the other kinds of injustice – unbelief, perversity, disobedience. All that God has forbidden is a wrongdoing, whether it relates to a right of God only or a right of His servants or of both.[1] What He has commanded as a turning away through abandoning and renouncing, as also of the turning away under the head of chastisement and penalty, is only [to be enforced] when there is no interest for the religion thereby that would be preponderant over its enforcement.[2] Otherwise, when in a

---

1 On the typology of rights in Ibn Taymiyya, see LAOUST, *Essai sur les doctrines*, 320–21.

2 'That the unbeliever lose his senses is better for him and for the Muslims. For him, it is [so] because that does not turn him from the remembrance of God and from the prayer but, rather, from unbelief and perversity. For the Muslims, it is [so] because drunkenness provokes enmity and hatred among the [unbelievers], and such [discords among them] are to the advantage of the Muslims. [To say] this is not to authorize wine or drunkenness but to rebuff the worse of two evils by the lesser [of them].

'That is why I commanded our companions not to forbid wine to the enemies of the Muslims – the Tatars, the Georgians and their likes. When they drink, I said to them, that does not turn them from the remembrance of God or from the prayer but, rather, from unbelief and from [spreading] corruption over the earth. Besides, that provokes enmity and hatred among them, and this is, for the Muslims, in [their] general interest (*maṣlaḥa*). Their being sober is worse than their being drunk. Thus there is nothing of good [to be gained] by helping them to be sober. Rather, it is preferable, [even] obligatory, to rebuff the evil that

bad deed there is a preponderance of goodness, it is not a bad deed.[1] And when there is in the chastisement, relatively to the crime, a source of preponderant corruption, [chastisement] is not a good thing but, quite the contrary, a bad one. If there is an equivalence [of good and bad in the outcome] it is neither a good thing nor a bad one.

PRAGMATISM AND THE MIDDLE WAY

What is aimed at by quitting (*hijrān*) may be abandonment of the bad deed of innovation, which is a wrong, a fault, a sin and an agent of corruption. What is aimed at by that may also be to accomplish a good deed [such as is constituted by] jihād, the forbidding of the reprehensible and the chastisement of the unjust, so that they may be restrained and repressed, and so that faith and virtuous deeds may be strengthened among the practitioners of these. Chastisement of an unjust one indeed dissuades souls from being unjust like him and encourages them to act in a manner contrary to his

---

these people [represent] by the expedient that is feasible, like drunkenness, etc.' (IBN TAYMIYYA, *al-Istiqāma*, ii. 165–66)
On this event, and more generally, on the utilitarianism of Ibn Taymiyya in matters of morality, see COOK, *Commanding Right and Forbidding Wrong in Islamic Thought* (2000), 154–55. See also the text translated above, p. 52, in which Ibn Taymiyya cautions against forbidding wine to a newly converted king who drinks, for fear of his apostasizing.

1 That is the case for example when the bad deed is followed by repentance. 'When [a believer] repents of [his acts of disobedience], that which the repentance follows is a good. To repent is indeed a good deed (*ḥasana*), which is among the good deeds most loved of God.' (IBN TAYMIYYA, *Majmūᶜ al-fatāwā*, trans. MICHOT, *Ibn Taymiyya: Un Dieu hésitant?*, 18–19)

injustice, whether in respect of faith or of the Tradition (*sunna*), etc.

When, therefore, by turning away from someone there is neither restraining of anyone nor renunciation by anyone but, to the contrary, a fading away of many of the good works that are commanded [to be done], it is not commanded [to us] to turn away from him.

Aḥmad [b. Ḥanbal] has mentioned this [in saying], about the people of Khurāsān of that period, that they would not be of [sufficient] strength to fight the Jahmīs. Given that they were incapable of showing enmity to them, the order to accomplish this good work lapsed. Accommodating to them in this regard was the [way to] push away the harm from the powerless believer. Perhaps it might also [entail merely] compromising with the powerful perverted ones. Similarly for [the doctrine of] power [of man over his deeds] (*qadar*), which had numerous partisans among the people of Baṣra: if, on account of this [doctrine], one had ceased to narrate ḥadīths from [those Baṣrans], the knowledge, the traditions (*sunna*) and the reports (*athar*) preserved among them would have disappeared.

When implementing the obligations related to [obtaining] knowledge, to [waging] jihād, etc. is difficult otherwise than by [recourse to] someone in whom there is innovation (*bidʿa*), the harm of which is less than the harm from abandonment of that obligation, then realizing the interest [from implementation] of the obligation with its accompanying factor of corruption, while [this interest] is preponderant over it, is better than the reverse.[1]

That is why the issues concerning these questions involve detail. Many of the answers from Imām Aḥmad [b. Ḥanbal] and other imāms are responding to the query of a questioner whose situation was known to the [imām] being asked, or they are addressing a person of particular (*muʿayyan*) identity, whose situation was known to [the imām being asked]. [These answers] are thus equivalent to the judgements emanating from the Messenger, may God pray over him and grant him peace, on concrete cases: what they stipulated is valid only for similar cases.

[However,] some people made of that [something] general. They made of [the principle entailing] turning away from and repudiating someone a [general] practice that they had not been commanded to do, and which was neither obligatory nor [even] preferable. Perhaps indeed they abandoned thereby

---

1 It would be useful to compare this passage to what Ibn Taymiyya wrote, perhaps thinking also of himself, on celibacy among certain scholars: see MICHOT, 'Un célibataire endurci', 186–67. Although he considers that renouncing marriage may be the price to be paid for leading a life devoted to knowledge and religion, he severely condemns whoever might claim to find in music, in dance, in alcohol and drugs, aids to a return to religious life, to spiritual quest or ecstasy. See the texts translated in MICHOT, *Ibn Taymiyya. Le Haschich et l'extase* (2001). In this regard what goes for a bibulous king newly converted to Islam is not automatically valid for society in general. And vice versa. Once again, everything is a matter of judgement and valuation.

some obligations and preferable works, and achieved thereby some forbidden things.

Some others for their part totally turned their backs on that. They did not turn away from what was commanded to them, such as evil deeds, innovations, [etc.]. On the contrary, they abandoned them by [simply] turning their backs on them, not as one would abandon them who renounced and hated [them]. Or indeed they [themselves] lapsed therein. It may also be that they abandon them by renouncing and hating [them], but they do not forbid them to others nor punish, by turning away from them, etc., people who were deserving of punishment for having given themselves over to [those things]. In respect of forbidding the reprehensible, they will have thus barred themselves from [doing] what they were commanded to do as obligatory or as preferable [actions].

They are [trapped] therefore between doing something that is reprehensible and ceasing to prohibit it – the former [amounts to] doing something that is prohibited to them, and [the latter to] abandoning something that they have been commanded. The former [thus amounts to] the latter. Now the religion of God is a just balance between that in which one goes too far (*al-ghālī fī-hi*) and that which one abuses (*al-jāfī ʿan-hu*).

And God, Praised is He, knows better!

Six Modern Readings

A. MUḤAMMAD ʿABD AL-SALĀM FARAJ

Extracts from *The Neglected Duty* (1981)[1]

THE DOMAIN IN WHICH WE ARE LIVING. A question arises here: are we living in an Islamic State? Among the conditions [to be fulfilled by such a] State is being governed by the institutions of Islam (*aḥkām al-islām*).

Imām Abū Ḥanīfa[2] stated in a fatwa that the domain of Islam changes into a domain of unbelief when three conditions combine: 1) being governed by the institutions of unbelief; 2) disappearance of security (*amān*) for the Muslims; 3) being a borderland [territory] or adjacent [to the frontiers] – this, on account of the fact that this domain is adjacent to the domain of unbelief, so much so that it is a source of

---

1 FARAJ, *al-Farīḍat al-ghāʾiba* (1981), here in the version from the internet site www.alkalema.us/algehad, which appears to be more accurate than the versions found in AḤMED, *al-Nabī al-musallaḥ, I: al-Rāfiḍūn. The Militant Prophet, I – The Rejectionists* (1991), 129, 132, and in ZAQZŪQ (ed.) *al-Fatāwā* (1997), x. 3764, 3768. Cf. the translations, following those versions, of JANSEN, *The Neglected Duty*, 166–67, 175–76, and of KEPEL, *Prophète et Pharaon*, 211–12.

2 Abū Ḥanīfa l-Nuʿmān b. Thābit (d. 150/767), theologian and jurist, eponymous founder of one of the four Sunnī rites. See J. Schacht, *EI²* art. 'Abū Ḥanīfa'.

danger for the Muslims and a reason for the disappearance of security.

Imām Muḥammad [b. al-Ḥasan][1] and Imām Abū Yūsuf,[2] the two companions of Abū Ḥanīfa, stated in a fatwa that the status (*ḥukm*) of a domain follows from the institutions that govern it.[3] If the institutions that govern it are the institutions of Islam, it is domain of Islam. If the institutions that govern it are institutions of unbelief, it is a domain of unbelief.

A land called Mardin had been governed according to the institutional regime (*ḥukm*) of Islam, subsequently power was taken over by people who implemented (*aqāma*) the institutional regime of unbelief. When Shaykh al-Islām Ibn Taymiyya was asked about it, if it was a domain of war or of peace, he replied stating [this] in a fatwa (in his book *The Fatwas*, xxviii. 241[4]):

This [city has a status that is] composite (murakkab), *in which both the things signified by [those terms are to be found]. It is not in the situation of a domain of peace in which the institutions* (aḥkām) *of Islam are implemented because its army* (jund) *is [composed of]*

---

1 Abū ʿAbd Allāh Muḥammad b. al-Ḥasan al-Shaybānī (d. 189/805), immediate disciple of Abū Ḥanīfa and a major jurist of his school. See É. Chaumont, *EI²* art. 'al-S͟haybānī'.

2 Abū Yūsuf b. Ibrāhīm al-Anṣārī (d. 182/798), immediate disciple of Abū Ḥanīfa and a major jurist of his school. See J. Schacht, *EI²* art. 'Abū Yūsuf'.

3 On the conditions under which, according to Abū Ḥanīfa and his two disciples, a domain of Islam changes into a domain of war, see AL-SHAYBĀNĪ, *al-Siyar*, trans. ḤĀMIDULLĀH, *al-Shaybānī: Le grand livre de la conduite de l'État*, i. 175.

4 The reference as given in the text here translated.

Muslims. Nor is it in the situation of a domain of war, whose inhabitants are unbelievers. Rather, it constitutes a third type [of domain], in which the Muslim shall be treated as he merits, and in which the one who departs from the Way/Law of Islam shall be combated as he merits.

Mardin[1]

The truth is that whoever looks closely at these sayings will not affirm any contradiction between the sayings of the imāms ...[2] Abū Ḥanīfa and his two companions did not

---

1 From DEWEY, 'Mardin in Mesopotamia' (1889), 4–5. See also: GUEST, *The Yezidis: A Study in Survival, Mesopotamia, Chaldea and Armenia* (n.d.), 110; SEVİM, 'Gravürlerle Türkiye' (2002), ii. 142.

2 Faraj understands Ibn Taymiyya's words – '[Mardin] is not in the situation of a domain of war either, whose inhabitants are unbelievers' – as meaning: 'Mardin is a domain of war although its inhabitants are Muslims.' That is the only reason why the

mention that the inhabitants [of the domain of war] are unbelievers… The Muslim who merits peace indeed does not merit war in the same way as the State [which] is, in spite of the fact that most of its inhabitants are Muslims, governed by the institutions of unbelief.

TO GOVERN BY MEANS OF ANYTHING OTHER THAN WHAT GOD HAS SENT DOWN [AS LAW]. The institutions that govern the Muslims today are institutions of unbelief. Furthermore, they are laws (*qānūn*) that the unbelievers have invented and according to which they lead the Muslims. Now God, Glorified and Exalted is He, has said: 'Those who do not govern by means of that which God has sent down, those are the unbelievers' (*al-Māʾida*, 5. 44). After the final demise of the caliphate in 1924, the extirpation of all the institutions of Islam, and the replacement of them by institutions that unbelievers have invented, their situation has become the very situation of the Tatars.[1] […]

---

opinion of the Damascene theologian can appear to him to correspond to that of those Ḥanafī jurists who speak of a domain of war without the condition that such a domain must be inhabited by unbelievers. Faraj in fact misunderstands Ibn Taymiyya, whose litigious phrasing means that, in order to have a domain of war, its inhabitants must be unbelievers.

1 That is to say, more accurately, the situation of the countries invaded by the Tatars in the period of Ibn Taymiyya. See the texts in which Ibn Taymiyya and Ibn Kathīr accuse the Mongols of preferring to manage their affairs according to the *Yāsā*, the great law of Genghis Khan, rather than according to 'the rule of God and His Messenger', in MICHOT, 'Textes spirituels XIII', 25–26, n. 7. For the disciple of the Shaykh al-Islām, 'whoever does that is an unbeliever, whom it is necessary to

fight until he comes back to the rule of God and of His Messenger': IBN KATHĪR, *Tafsīr al-Qurʾān al-ʿaẓīm* (1990), ii. 64, trans. in MICHOT, 'Textes spirituels XIII', 26, n. 7. See also, among other studies: SIVAN, 'Ibn Taymiyya: Father of the Islamic Revolution', 43.

The other great disciple of Ibn Taymiyya, Ibn Qayyim al-Jawziyya, takes a more open approach that plainly deserves to be attended to: 'A Shāfiʿī said: "No politics (*siyāsa*) excepting something that corresponds with the Law (*sharʿ*)!" And Ibn ʿAqīl [d. 513/1120] said: "Politics is a thing that is in fact such that, through it, people are closer to virtue and further from corruption, even though the Messenger did not institute [it] and no revelation brought it [down to this world] here-below." If in saying "excepting something that corresponds with the Law (*sharʿ*)" you mean "which does not run against what the Law has pronounced upon", it is correct. If [on the other hand] you mean [by that] "No politics except for what the Law has pronounced upon", it is an error and it [entails] accusing of error the Companions [of the Prophet...]. God, Praised is He, sent His Messengers and sent down His Books so that people should strictly practise equity (*qisṭ*) [see Qurʾān, *al-Ḥadīd*, 57. 25], meaning the justice (*ʿadl*) by which the earth and the heavens subsist. When the signs (*amāra*) of justice appear and its face is radiant, by whatever means it may be, there [you find] the Law of God and His religion. God, Praised is He, is too aware, too wise and too just to restrict the ways of justice, its signs and its marks, to a single thing, to then reject something that may be more evident than those [and] provide a stronger demonstration [and] clearer sign [of justice], to not include it among them, and to not judge, when such a thing exists and subsists, that it is obligatory. Through the ways that He has instituted as Law, He has rather, Praised is He, made it plain that what is aimed at by Him is that justice be made to rule among His servants and that people strictly practise equity. Whatever the ways by which justice and equity obtain, they are a part of the religion and do not run against it.' IBN QAYYIM

A GROUP OF THE FATWAS OF IBN TAYMIYYA THAT ARE USEFUL IN THIS TIME. It is sufficient then to transcribe certain of the fatwas of Ibn Taymiyya on the status of such people… We have already mentioned his fatwa on the status of the city of Mardin, which the Tatars were governing by means of laws (*qānūn*) combining some elements of the Law (*sharīᶜa*) of the Jews and the Nazarenes with a part of Islam and a part of Jewish reasoning. He said:

In regard to being a domain of war or of peace, it is [a city of a status] composite (murakkab), *in which both the things signified by [those terms are to be found]. It is not in the situation of a domain of peace in which the institutions* (aḥkām) *of Islam are implemented because its army* (jund) *is [composed of] Muslims. Nor is it in the situation of a domain of war, whose inhabitants are unbelievers. Rather, it constitutes a third type [of domain], in which the Muslim shall be treated as he merits, and in which the one who departs from the Way/Law of Islam shall be combated as he merits.* (end, vol. 28, p. 241[1])

WHAT IS THE STATUS OF THE HELP AND ASSISTANCE THAT MIGHT BE GIVEN TO THEM? Shaykh al-Islām Ibn Taymiyya said, in response to this question: (p. 240 of the *Book of Jihād*[2])

To give assistance to those who depart from the Way/Law of the religion of Islam (sharīᶜa) *is also forbidden, whether it be the people of Mardin or others.*

AL-JAWZIYYA, *al-Ṭuruq al-ḥikmiyya fī l-siyāsat al-sharᶜiyya* (2002), 17–18.

In which of these two disciples would the Damascene theologian more readily have recognized himself?

1 The reference as given in the text here translated.

2 The reference as given in the text here translated.

If the one resident [in Mardin] is disabled from putting his religion into effect (iqāma), *it is obligatory for him to emigrate. If that is not [the case], it [remains] preferable [but] is not obligatory.*
That [these people] give assistance to the enemy of the Muslims with their persons or their property is forbidden to them, and they must abstain therefrom by all the means possible to them: evading, equivocating, compromising. When it is not possible for them to do this except by emigrating, [emigrating] is incumbent on every single one of them.

And Ibn Taymiyya added, having in mind the inhabitants of Mardin who help the Tatars, the governing power –

It is not lawful to insult them in a general manner, nor to accuse them of hypocrisy [hiding unbelief]. Rather, insulting and accusing of hypocrisy is to be done in respect of the specific characteristics mentioned in the Book and the Sunna. Now this concerns the people of Mardin and others also.

– meaning, not all of them.

B. ᶜABD ALLĀH ᶜAZZĀM

Extracts from *Declaration of Jihād* (1988?)[1]

THE TRANSFORMATION OF A DOMAIN, FROM DOMAIN OF ISLAM TO DOMAIN OF WAR. From what we have recalled it appears that the precise scale [to use] in order to know [the status of] a domain is the law (*qānūn*). If sovereignty (*siyāda*) belongs [therein] to the Islamic law, a domain is domain of

---

1 ᶜAZZĀM, *Iᶜlān al-jihād.*

Islam. If sovereignty belongs [therein] to another law, whatever this law may be, it is a domain of war; even when the inhabitants [thereof] are Muslims […]

When a domain is Islamic, the Islamic Law (*sharīʿa*) rules there, decision (*ḥukm*) therein belongs to the law of God and the rulers therein are Muslims applying this Law. Accordingly, every Muslim owes loyalty and love to such a domain.

When on the other hand a domain is domain of Islam and some people make themselves masters thereof and reduce to nothing the Legislation (*sharʿ*) of God, apply therein another legislation, constructed by the caprices of human beings, or mix the Legislation of God with the legislations of human beings and implement the latter, this domain no longer remains domain of Islam.

But what is the name of such a domain after the Legislation of God therein has been reduced to nothing?

The majority of the scholar-jurists have said that it is a domain of war […] and such is the opinion of Mālik [b. Anas],[1] of al-Shāfiʿī,[2] of Aḥmad [b. Ḥanbal] and, among the Ḥanafis, of the two companions[3] [of Abū Ḥanīfa]. A domain becomes, they indeed said, domain of war merely from the fact that the institutions (*aḥkām*) of associationism (*shirk*) are

---

1 Mālik b. Anas (d. 179/795), theologian and jurist, eponymous founder of one of the four Sunnī rites. See J. Schacht, *EI*[2] art. 'Mālik b. Anas'.

2 Muḥammad b. Idrīs al-Shāfiʿī, Abū ʿAbd Allāh (d. 205/820), jurist and eponymous founder of one of the four Sunnī rites. See É. Chaumont, *EI*[2] art. 'al-Shāfiʿī'.

3 Muḥammad b. al-Ḥasan al-Shaybānī and Abū Yūsuf Yaʿqūb b. Ibrāhīm al-Anṣārī; see above, p. 102, nn. 1, 2.

implemented therein. The coming-to-be of Islam is correlative to the coming-to-be of its institutions. When, therefore, these institutions disappear from a [domain], it no longer remains domain of Islam.

ᶜAbd Allāh ᶜAzzām

As for Imām Abū Ḥanīfa, he held an opinion different from his two companions, Abū Yūsuf and Muḥammad b. al-Ḥasan, and said that a domain of Islam does not become domain of war except on three conditions: *a*) the coming-to-be of the institutions of unbelief and their implementation; *b*) being a land bordering on the domain of unbelief, [that is to say] of war; *c*) that neither any Muslim nor any protected person (*dhimmī*) is in security, [that they no longer enjoy therein] the security that they used to enjoy, namely the primary security that the Legislation [of God] assures to the Muslims and that the Legislation [of God] assures to the protected person by the contract of protection (*dhimma*).

According to the opinion of the majority of the jurist-scholars – the Mālikīs, the Shāfiᶜīs, Aḥmad [b. Ḥanbal] and, among the Ḥanafīs, the two companions [of Abū Ḥanīfa] – the Islamic regions that are governed by means of anything other than that which God sent down [as Law] are no longer counted as domain of Islam but, on the contrary, become domain of war [...] It is also the opinion of Professor Abū Zahra.[1]

As for Ibn Taymiyya, he held the view that it is a third [sort of] domain – [this] domain where the Legislation of God used to be sovereign and where, subsequently, the institutional regime was changed by a positive law, [one] of human invention. Such a domain has ceased to be a domain of Islam but has not become a domain of war. It is a third [sort of] domain. As example of such a domain, Ibn Taymiyya suggested Mardin, which was part of the domain of Islam, where the Legislation of God was implemented, and of which a group of unbelievers later made themselves masters, who reduced to nothing [therein] the Legislation of God. [...]

THE OPINIONS OF THE AFGHAN ULEMA ON KABUL, NOW (UNDER THE GOVERNMENT OF NAJĪB[2] OR WHILE IT IS GOVERNED BY THE RUSSIANS). The points of view of the Afghan ulema on the government of Afghanistan now differ: is it a domain of war or a domain of Islam? The most well-known things said [on this subject] form two opinions:

---

1 Muḥammad Abū Zahra (1898–1974), professor at al-Azhar and the University of Cairo, one of the most influential academic authorities in twentieth-century Islam. The long list of his works includes studies on *fiqh*, the four imāms, Ibn Taymiyya, Shīʿism, comparative religion, the concept of war in Islam.

2 Muḥammad Najībullāh (1947–96), Communist leader, head of the secret services of Afghanistan (1980–87), then head of state (1987–92) during the Soviet occupation (end 1979–1989) and until the proclamation of the Islamic republic by the Mujāhidīn. Hanged by the Ṭalibān when they took Kabul.

The first opinion, which is the opinion of the majority of the ulema of Afghanistan, is that Kabul has not changed from domain of Islam to domain of war. They take their cue from the above-mentioned opinion of Abū Ḥanīfa, who imposes three conditions [...] They hold that the third condition has not been realized and that, in consequence, Kabul has not become domain of war. It is the opinion of the majority of the ulema of the north of Afghanistan.

The second opinion, which is the opinion of certain ulema of the south of Afghanistan, is that Afghanistan is domain of war. Consequently, they have issued a fatwa suspending the Friday prayer in [its] mosques. It seems that they take their cue from the opinion of the two companions [of Abū Ḥanīfa], namely Abū Yūsuf and Muḥammad b. al-Ḥasan.

We ourselves hold that Afghanistan is a third [sort of] domain, like Mardin: it is not domain of Islam, nor yet is it a domain of unbelief, a domain of war, since some institutions of the domain of Islam and some institutions of the domain of war are implemented there.

C. MUḤAMMAD AL-MASᶜARĪ

Extracts from *The Definitive Proofs of the [Religious] Illegitimacy of the Saudi State* (1995)[1]

The condition under which a domain remains domain of Islam is to be governed (*ḥukm*) by Islam and that one enjoys therein the security [provided by] the Muslims. When these

[1] AL-MASᶜARĪ, *al-Adillat al-qaṭᶜiyya ᶜalā ᶜadam sharᶜiyyat al-dawlat al-saᶜūdiyya* (1997).

two matters are not guaranteed, a domain remains domain of unbelief. To be governed by Islam and to enjoy the security [provided by] the Muslims are two matters that necessarily go together.

As for characterizing a 'country' as 'an Islamic country' or as 'an Islamic region' or, in a similar way, [to speak] in the plural of 'Islamic countries' or 'Islamic kingdoms' or even of 'the Islamic world', etc., that is to be done pursuant to one of the following considerations:

1) That most of the inhabitants are Muslims, with no account taken of the institutional regime and [of the type of] security that [exists] therein.

2) By considering the system of government or the security that [exists] therein: if it is a domain of Islam, it is valid from this point of view to call it 'Islamic'.

3) By considering its past. If [this country] has been, in the past, governed by Islam, for instance as in Andalusia or Palestine, it is Islamic with regard to the fact that Islam ruled over its territory in an earlier time. To take into consideration its being presently governed by unbelief is Legally to be refused, even if [that] is a fact, a reality. For indeed Islam is to hold the upper hand, not be subject to [it]. Jihād with a view to recovering [such] a [country] remains a duty upon the individual. However, this does not mean that [such] a [country] is a domain of Islam, or that it deserves to be called 'domain of Islam', or that one should call it 'domain of Islam' in order to insist upon the obligation to take it back from the unbelievers. The obligation to recover it is a judgement of the Law [firmly] established for this particular situation, and one that has no connection with the characterization of the

domain, nor with the fact that jihād [for recovering it] is an individual duty or a collective duty.

[To characterize a country or a world as Islamic] may also be done for other good considerations, different from those. Even though such characterizations may have a certain link with Islam or the domain of Islam, they nevertheless do not correspond to the concept of domain of Islam. Or, rather, they are in contradiction with it in the case where a country is governed by unbelief even though it is an Islamic country given that most of its inhabitants are Muslims: the country is thus an Islamic country although the domain is a domain of unbelief.

It is to such considerations – about a country that is governed according to the institutions of unbelief whereas its inhabitants are Muslims – that Shaykh al-Islām Ibn Taymiyya applied himself in the Mardin fatwa. [He said in that fatwa] that in the land of Mardin, which had fallen under the rule of the unbelieving Tatars, that there were [some things related] to what one means by domain of Islam and similarly [some things related] to what one means by domain of unbelief.

Thus, he said, in response to a group of questions about Mardin:

QUESTION on the land of Mardin [...] [1]

Note the distinction that [Ibn Taymiyya applies] – God have mercy on him – between the characterization of the domain and the statuses of the persons of its inhabitants.

---

1 The full text of the Mardin fatwa is given here. See the translation of it above, Text I, pp. 63–65.

[Note] similarly that he makes the enjoyment of the security [provided by] the Muslims a condition – where he says '…because its army (*jund*) is [composed of] Muslims' – in addition to the fact that [the city] should be governed by Islam. This being so, he was not accurate – God have mercy on him – in considering the domain [of Mardin] as [being of] composite [status]. This domain was, to be sure, adjacent to unbelief, albeit that the land was, at the same time, an Islamic country, the majority of whose inhabitants were Muslims. Now, the statuses of a domain and its characterizations are not necessarily the statuses of its inhabitants or the characterization [that one gives] to them, as will be stated in detail later.

The outcome [of all this] is that the fact that a domain is a domain of unbelief or a domain of Islam depends on the actual (*wāqiʿ*) reality of this domain […]. What makes this even clearer is that the Muslims are commanded to make war, that is, to fight, until people say 'No god except God,' or until they submit to the institutions of Islam. If they submit to the institutions of Islam, there is no further [duty or need] to fight them, even when they continue to be unbelievers, unresponsive to the call (*daʿwa*) [to convert]. The reason for the cessation [of hostility] is their accepting to be governed by Islam. Thus, when they are governed by Islam, their lands are then changed from domain of war to domain of Islam. The cessation of war or its continuance thus depend on the fact of being governed by Islam or not, which demonstrates that the qualifying characteristic that decides the fact, for a domain, of being domain of Islam or domain of unbelief, is [its] being governed by Islam. And the fact, for [Islam], of being governing (*ḥukm*), that is to say [of being] in power (*sulṭān*), has the meaning that internal and external security are [provided] by it, that is, by the power of Islam. If this is not the case, it loses the particular characteristic because of which it is described as a government (*ḥukm*). In consequence, being governed by Islam, and the security which is one of the necessary concomitants of that are the two [things] that determine whether a domain may be described as domain of Islam or domain of war.

D. ᶜABD AL-ᶜAZĪZ AL-JARBŪᶜ

Extract from *The Book Informing of the Obligation to Emigrate from the Domain of Unbelief to the Domain of Islam* (2001)[1]

The situation that I wish to speak about [...] is not [that of] the preferable or recommended emigration, leading from a land of innovation to a [place] where there is not innovation, nor from a land of perversion and disobedience to a land which is not like that, but only [the emigration] from a domain of unbelief to a domain of Islam. More precisely, [I wish to speak of the emigration whereby one quits] a land whose inhabitants are Muslims but where the institutional system is apostate. That is to say, a land whose inhabitants are Muslims and the majority of whose visible institutions of government are Islam[ic], [but where] unbelief is manifest to those who seek knowledge and those who have that status,

---

1 AL-JARBŪᶜ, *Kitāb al-Iᶜlām bi-wujūb al-hijra min dār al-kufr ilā dār al-islām* (2001).

though the people do not know it on account of the fact that the ulema and others disguise [the reality], and of the fact also of their ignorance of the religion of God, Exalted is He. This will become plain from the following example.

If we take for example one of the Arab countries...the populace are Muslim all together. Further, the mosques are packed. They observe the Friday prayers, and the daily prayer in congregation. The sound of the call to prayer fills the air the whole time. Nevertheless, the rulers rule this populace by means of positive laws mendaciously and falsely called 'Islamic', or 'derived from Islam', according to their claim. Similarly, the courts are positive and the methods of teaching secularized. To make public that one detests the unbelievers, and [would] have nothing to do with them and their religion, is a crime that the regime forbids to you. The jihād is reduced to nothing. Any individual about whom it is established that one day he led a jihād is chastised. To be friends of the unbelievers and to help them against the Muslims and... and... and... [other] facts that the tongue is incapable of describing. And what makes things worse, and still more confused, is that a band – the dregs – of the ulema of the government bleat from morning to night, saying of these holders of authority that it is obligatory to obey them and to fall in line with them: [that] the one who does not do so will indeed die a death [worthy] of the age of Ignorance!!!

Here the big question interposes itself: what is the status of these domains, of which such are the characteristics? And what is the status of emigration (*hijra*) [parting] from these domains in such a situation, when the Muslim is no longer capable in such domains of openly (*iẓhār*) practising his religion?

Banner of the internet site of Shaykh al-Jarbūʿ[1]

ANSWER. There can be no doubt that the status of such a domain [is that it] is no longer Muslim. It is only a domain of unbelief or a composite domain, as Shaykh al-Islām Ibn Taymiyya said of the land of Mardin [...]. I incline toward the opinion of Shaykh al-Islām Ibn Taymiyya – God have mercy on him – in this: such a domain appeared in his time, whose situation was that determined by events, and he strove (*ijtahada*) – God have mercy on him – to realize the way to characterize a domain like that. At any rate, the difference [between the statuses of domain of unbelief and composite domain] is [purely] verbal, if we examine the status of emigration [parting] from such a domain. Those who say it is a domain of unbelief and those who say it is a composite domain indeed agree in speaking of the obligation, on whoever is not capable of openly practising his religion [therein], to emigrate from it. An insignificant number of Ḥanafīs are [the] only [ones to hold] a different opinion on this matter.

---

1 *www.geocities.com/aljarbo/alrsail.htm*

E. ZUHAYR SĀLIM

Extracts from *Positions on the Law of Jihād* [1]

DOMAIN OF WAR, DOMAIN OF ISLAM: A STRATEGIC DIVISION IN PAST HISTORY. The division of the world into domain of Islam, domain of war, and domain of pact, that the former jurists applied during past centuries derived simply from a concrete reality, governed by the circumstances and international usages prevalent in those times. The development of international systems and laws, the signature of pacts and treaties, which organize the life of nations and peoples in a way that serves the cause of man and corresponds to the spirit of Islam in [its] rejection of dissension (*fitna*), and the opening up of spaces for the liberty of man and the call [to embrace Islam] (*daʿwa*) – all that makes a demand on Muslim jurists to re-examine the former divisions, which were above all conjunctural and circumstantial.

Among the things that makes it certain that such a division was purely relative (*iʿtibārī*), there is [the response of] Imām Ibn Taymiyya – may God, Exalted is He, have mercy on him – when he was questioned about the city of Mardin. It was one of the Syrian fortresses facing the Byzantines. Its population was mixed: some Muslims and some Christians. The administration of it passed sometimes to the Byzantines, sometimes to the Muslims. Ibn Taymiyya was asked about the status of this city and about the status of its inhabitants,

---

1 SĀLIM, *Waqfāt fī fiqh al-jihād.*

who found themselves at one time under the authority of the Muslims, and at another under the authority of the Christian Byzantines. Was it a domain of war or a domain of Islam? He answered…, and we shall transcribe here in full the question and the answer, because they constitute kinds of profitable and useful juristic reflection.

[Ibn Taymiyya] – God have mercy on him – was asked about the land of Mardin […][1]

Banner of the internet site of Zuhayr Sālim[2]

What this fatwa makes certain is the relative character of the division [of the world] into domain of war and domain of Islam, and that the appearance of any new international

---

1 The full text of the Mardin fatwa is given here. See the translation of it above, Text I, pp. 63–65.

2 *www.alsharqalrabi.org.uk.*

situation demands from the evolution of Islamic law some shift to a new division.

For the jurists, the domain of Islam is that where the Muslim is secure in respect of his religion, his person, his property and his dignity, where the rites of Islam are observed and where its prescriptions are implemented. The domain of war, or the domain of unbelief, is that where the Muslim is not secure in respect of his religion, his person, his property and his dignity, where the rites of Islam are not observed and where its prescriptions are not implemented. The domain of Islam is not only the one where most of the inhabitants are Muslims; and the domain of unbelief is not only the one where most of the inhabitants are unbelievers.

The historical division hinged on two elements: security, and the nature of the regime in power, [determined] according to the public practice of the rites and the implementation of the prescriptions. Any reflection on the nature of the world today, in the light of the current international situation, will assuredly lead to [the conclusion] that a new reality has been set in place, or to new divisions, on the line of what Ibn Taymiyya alluded to in his argument on the city of Mardin.

Shall we be capable of re-dividing the world of today into 'domain of the call' (*dār daʿwa*), where the Muslim is secure in respect of his religion, his person, his property, and finds a perfect liberty to call to the religion of God, and 'domain of dissensions' (*dār fitna*), where the Muslim is exposed to various sorts of ill-will and hostility on account of his religion and his belief, or because he takes on the duty laid upon him to call [people to the religion of God]? If such a division is acceptable, what is required of the Muslim, in the two situations, is to lead himself to the road of wisdom in order to push back the ill-will and to contain the dissensions, or in order to issue his call and guide people toward the religion of God.

Those who hold to a historical division of the present international reality, by linking the historical and the religious and by passing over the present reality and its new facts in all their dimensions, civic, political, and related to the call [to go toward God], unconsciously commit a strategic blunder and, vis-à-vis the Law, a major error.

Besides, those who hold [that it is right] to divide the world into domain of unbelief and domain of Islam, then to put many of the Muslims' countries together in the first category, as a pretext for making it lawful [to spill] the blood of people and [to deprive them] of their property, commit something forbidden by the Law [...]

For sure, the ideological and political liberation to which the world of today is witness constitutes a space inviting the Muslim who would act to project the words of God into the hearts of the people and [into] their heads. Certainly, a good word [placed] in a good heart is a thousand times better than stray bullets fired from here and there. 'He is the One who has sent His Messenger with the guidance and the religion of the Real in order to make it appear above all religion' (Qurʾān, *al-Tawba*, 9. 33).

F. SAꜤD AL-DĪN AL-KIBBĪ

Extract from *Whereby One Makes the Servants [of God] See, by Discovering the Truth about Certain Questions on the Jihād* [1]

If fighting had been an obligation that is constant – at [every] step, and in [every] situation, in [every] time and in [every] place, fighting would have been made obligatory or preferable for the weak, and not emigration. Now this is what Shaykh al-Islām [Ibn Taymiyya] issued as a fatwa for the people of Mardin – a land that was, in former times, the nearest to our present reality – he said: *If the one resident [in Mardin] is disabled from putting his religion into effect* (iqāma), *it is obligatory for him to emigrate. If that is not [the case], it [remains] preferable [but] is not obligatory.*

'It is obligatory for him to emigrate…'[2]

---

1 AL-KIBBĪ, *Tabṣīr al-ʿibād bi-taḥqīq baʿḍ masāʾil al-jihād.*

2 *Blacas* ewer, Mosul (Iraq), 629/1232.

AFTERWORD

Crass howlers about Ibn Taymiyya have long been in circulation – one might think as far back as the tittle-tattle about him hawked around by Ibn Baṭṭūṭa.[1] Since 9/11, however, the situation has worsened. The most ignorant untruths are reproducing apace, not only in the media but even in supposedly serious studies. Some examples:

N. J. Delong-Bas, of Georgetown University, reproaches Ibn Taymiyya for 'his espousal of the division of the world into two absolute and mutually exclusive spheres – the land of Islam (*dar al-islam*) and the land of unbelief (*dar al-kufr*) – which for him described both a status (Muslim versus unbeliever) and a necessarily hostile relationship between the two.'[2] According to Bernard Haykel, professor of Islamic Law at the University of New York: 'Ibn Taymiyya's importance lies in that he was willing to hereticize fellow Muslims who did not share his views and, more important, he declared per-

---

1 See LITTLE, 'Did Ibn Taymiyya Have a Screw Loose?' (1975), 95–96; ALLOUCHE, 'A Study of Ibn Baṭṭūṭah's Account of his 726/1326 Journey through Syria and Arabia' (1990), 284–90.

2 DELONG-BAS, *Wahhabi Islam: From Revival and Reform to Global Jihad* (2004), 248.

missible war against Muslim rulers who did not apply the Shari'ah (he advocated war against the Mongols who had declared themselves to be Muslims but did not apply Islamic law).'[1] Menahem Milson, professor of Arabic literature at the Hebrew University of Jerusalem, writes: 'according to Ibn Taymiyya, a Muslim ruler who commits grave sins or applies alien laws (i.e., non-Islamic laws) is no better than an apostate (*murtadd*) and should be put to death. Hence, waging *jihad* against such rulers is a religious duty.'[2] Much the same approach, but expressed with bulleted succinctness, is found on a French site, *Autonomie*, presenting itself as the site of 'the counter revolution (counter-neoliberal)': 'Already in Ibn Taymiyya, its theoretician, the *jihād* is before all else a call to tyrannicide.'[3]

The rosette for such ineptitude most probably goes, however, to Guy Sorman, reputed professor at the Institut des Sciences Politiques of the University of Paris. In a recent work he wrote:[4]

---

1 HAYKEL, 'Radical Salafism: Osama's Ideology', *Dawn* (2001).

2 MILSON, 'Reform *vs.* Islamism in the Arab World Today' (15 Sept. 2004).

3 AUTONOMIE, *Pendant les attentats, le bourrage de crâne continue* (Communiqué of 9th Nov. 2001).

4 SORMAN, *Les enfants de Rifaa: musulmans et modernes* (2003), 61–62. This passage is translated as follows by A. Puri in the English version of Guy Sorman's book, published in India: 'The Sufis, on the other hand, adapt to any power structure as long as it is opposed to disorder whereas fundamentalism does not exclude the right to revolt. Ibn Taymiyya was the first influential author to legitimize revolt. A contemporary of Ibn Khaldun, he was one of the last great Muslim philosophers and a critic of Aris-

While the Sufis have accommodated to any power provided it countered disorder, the fundamentalist current [in Islam] has not excluded the duty of rebellion. The first influential author to legitimize rebellion was Ibn Taymiyya, one of the last great Muslim philosophers, contemporary of Ibn Khaldūn, [and] critic of Aristotelian reason. However, beyond his philosophical works, he remains the initiator of a tradition of radical Islam uninterrupted since his time. He lived in Baghdād, was present at the fall of the ᶜAbbāsid caliphate in 1258 and its replacement by a Mongol dynasty. Was that dynasty not Muslim too? According to Ibn Taymiyya, those Mongols were Muslims only on the surface – they persisted in following the codes of their ancestors rather than the *Sharīᶜa* – pseudo-converts, '*marrano*'[1] Muslims! Ibn Taymiyya declared them apostates, which implied that every good Muslim should overthrow them. This fatwa inaugurated a theological and political

---

totelian logic. More than his philosophical work, he is known as the initiator of a radical Islamic tradition that lives on till this day. He lived in Baghdad and in 1258 witnessed the fall of the Abyssid [*sic*] Caliphate and the coming to power of a Mongol dynasty. Ibn Taymiyya dismissed the Mongols as fake Muslims —they followed their ancestral code rather than the sharia. He declared that they were apostates, so it became the duty of every good Muslim to overthrow them. This fatwa marked the beginning of a theological and political revolution: there is not a single fundamentalist Islamic movement that does not take its inspiration from his thought.' SORMAN, *The Children of Rifaa: In Search of a Moderate Islam* (2004), 51.

1 '*marrano*' is from the Spanish for 'pig', 'swine', a term of abuse formerly applied to Jews converted forcibly to Christianity, which gives the sense here, roughly, 'pig-eating Muslims'. It is inconceivable that Ibn Taymiyya could ever have answered 'Was that not a Muslim dynasty too?' in such words. On his argument for the Legal obligation to accept Muslims as they give themselves out to be, see above, p. 19 n. 2; p. 89 n. 2.

revolution: there is not a fundamentalist Islamic movement that does not refer back to it…

Now it is true that, in a text often attributed to Shams al-Dīn al-Dhahabī (d. 748/1348), Ibn Taymiyya is accused of having 'repeatedly swallowed the poison of the philosophers and their works.'[1] But to go from there to making him out to be 'one of the last great Muslim philosophers' is quite a jump. As for judging him to have been 'a contemporary of Ibn Khaldūn' – that is to be ignorant that he died in 728/1328 and that the Maghrebi thinker was not born until 732/1332. One need not take offence at so trite an error,[2] any more than at the statement that the great theologian of Damascus 'lived in Baghdād' (whereas he never went to Iraq), or that he 'was present at the fall of the ʿAbbāsid caliphate in 1258'

---

1 See MICHOT, 'Vanités intellectuelles… L'impasse des rationalismes selon… Ibn Taymiyya' (2000), 600.

2 Indeed, one would prefer to turn away, except that these errors inform general attitudes and prejudices, which in turn, with the most dire consequences, shape public policy. For example, the false notion that Ibn Taymiyya is the progenitor of violent modern Islamic radicalism finds its way into the US government's *9/11 Commission Report* (ch. 12, 362): 'The catastrophic threat at this moment in history is […] the threat posed by Islamist terrorism […] Usama Bin Ladin and other Islamist terrorist leaders draw on a long tradition of extreme intolerance within one stream of Islam (a minority tradition), from at least Ibn Taimiyyah, through the founders of Wahhabism, through the Muslim Brotherhood, to Sayyid Qutb. […] It is not a position with which Americans can bargain or negotiate. With it there is no common ground […] on which to begin a dialogue.'

(whereas he was not born until 661/1263)... One may excuse also the telescoping of a mere few decades that led to linking Ibn Taymiyya's anti-Mongol fatwas to the destruction of Baghdād by the unbelieving hordes of Hūlāgū in 1258, instead of to the invasions of Syria by Hūlāgū's successors (become Muslims in the interim), the īlkhāns Ghāzān and Öljāytū, in 700/1300 and the years following. Finally, one may pardon also the facile conflation by the brilliant professor of political philosophy of 'the duty of rebellion' against the authorities and the duty of resistance to an invader. If indeed Ibn Taymiyya declared the Tatars to be apostates, it was not so that all good Muslims 'should overthrow them', but rather so that they should take part in expelling them from Syria and pushing them back beyond the Euphrates...

What blossoming of knowledge dare one hope for if the water irrigating the groves of Academe springs from such a well of false science?[1] What may one expect from the new Orientalism, if it restricts itself to re-assuming for its own

---

1 Let us quote another two gems of this false science. There is, first of all, this definition of Wahhābism: 'This ideology had been theorized as soon as the 12th century by the Turk Ibn Taymiyya, who died in a Baghdadi gaol, condemned by the caliphs for his integrism [fundamentalism]' (ANONYMOUS, 'Le Wahhabisme' [25 Sept. 2001]. And from C. MONIQUET, *Le Djihad. Histoire secrète des hommes et des réseaux en Europe* (2004), 47–48: 'Ahmed Taqi el-Dinne ibn Taymiyya, jurist and theologian born in Damascus in 1236 [*sic*] and who died almost a centenarian (in a gaol) in 1328 [...] Ibn Taymiyya is at the origin of a concept which today justifies many jihadist actions; thus, a Muslim government which would not fully apply the Sharia will have to be fought as an apostate power.'

use, without the least effort of inquiry, the 'Mongolizing' over-simplifications of a certain brand of Islamism, and thereby grants to those over-simplifications a new lease of life? Are we to believe that an Ibn Taymiyya who does not fit among the most extreme of Islamists is no longer of interest to the Islamologists? Why? Is it because it must be so reassuring for them always to be able to rely on the theology of rebellion attributed to him? Because only in that way are they able to confirm (to anyone who might still be in doubt of it) the essentially anti-civic nature of Islam and its 'ragheads' and, following from that, their irreducible incompatibility with the values of the West and of modernity?[1]

---

1 J. J. G. JANSEN (in a recent study, which I thank him for sending to me) presents the anti-Mongol fatwas of the Shaykh al-Islām under the appropriate heading of 'theology of war' relative to 'a specific military conflict' (*De radicaal-islamitische ideologie: van Ibn Taymiyya tot Osama ben Laden* [2004], 6, 9). That said, he makes so little – as I explain above, p. 55 note – of the theologian's loyalty and quietism in regard to internal politics, that (to put it bluntly) he places his academic credentials on the side of the betrayal of Ibn Taymiyya's thought by 'Mongolizing' Islamism. This is all the more strange since he does know that Ibn Taymiyya condemned tyrannicide. In 1986 for example, he wrote: 'It would seem evident that religiously motivated tyrannicides could expect little support from Ibn Taymiyya, especially when their doctrines demonstrate so striking a similarity to the doctrines of the Khārijīs, who are so clearly […] condemned by Ibn Taymiyya' ('Ibn Taymiyyah and the Thirteenth Century: a Formative Period of Modern Muslim Radicalism' [1987–88], 393).
E. SIVAN, in 'Ibn Taymiyya: Father of the Islamic Revolution. Medieval Theology and Modern Politics' (1983, 43–44, 50) and in *Radical Islam. Medieval Theology and Modern Politics* (1990,

Let us allow, it may be objected, that Ibn Taymiyya indeed did not 'Mongolize' the Mamlūk sultan whose subject he was, and allow also that his thinking was not of a fundamentally political cast. But what then is the origin of the un-

---

98–100), presents a truly surprising example of 'Mongolizing' Orientalism. He is aware of the purpose of Ibn Taymiyya's anathematization of the Mongol invaders for their lapses from the *Sharīʿa*: to mobilize resistance against them. Nevertheless, he considers excommunication and the necessity of fighting against authorities who are insufficiently Muslim to have, for the theologian, a 'general doctrinal significance'. For proof of this he presents an extract from the *Siyāsa sharʿiyya* on the necessity of fighting against 'whoever departs from the law of Islam' (*al-Siyāsat al-sharʿiyya*, ed./trans. LAOUST, *Le traité de droit public d'Ibn Taymīya* [1990], 154/187). From that he concludes that, for Ibn Taymiyya, 'a Sunnī authority becomes illegitimate if it does not implement a substantial part of the *Sharīʿa*.' The problem is that this extract from the *Siyāsa* – to which Sivan refers in order to attribute to the Shaykh al-Islām this general theology of 'right of resistance to an illegitimate power (*Widerstandsrecht*)', and to make him out to be a promoter of 'active opposition to the authorities' – is explicitly concerned with rebellious minorities and therefore has nothing to do with any form whatever of internal opposition to the political power in place. Sivan then goes on to be surprised by Ibn Taymiyya's loyalty vis-à-vis the Mamlūks and offers a most unsatisfactory explanation for it. To be sure, he had already, without any exploration of the corpus of the theologian's works, affirmed that he had broken with the Sunnī tradition of quietism and pragmatic obedience to power. Nothing of this is of much substance. 'Mongolizing' Islamism proves itself to be a particularly contagious virus, the more formidable for seeming to attack the most basic immune defences of academic research: an inquiring mind, respect for texts, and critical prudence.

faithfulness to his thought and betrayal of his ideas, as set out in the foregoing pages? In other words, at what point does the politicization of Ibn Taymiyya begin, and who were the first Mongolizing Islamists? In so-called learned works, just as in the press, 'the usual suspect' is Muḥammad b. ʿAbd al-Wahhāb (d. 1206/1792).[1] To be more serious, the truth demands a humble recognition that, despite the works of Henri Laoust, Thomas Michel and Bashier M. Nafi,[2] a systematic and detailed historical study of the influences exerted by the Mamlūk Shaykh al-Islām on the seven centuries of Islamic thought after him, and a mapping of the channels that these influences have followed, remain tasks yet to be accomplished. Which of his two principal disciples, Ibn Kathīr and Ibn Qayyim al-Jawziyya, has in fact had the more decisive impact? When, and where, and according to what modalities? And what (to mention but one track unexplored by Laoust) of a reformist movement such as that, a hundred years before Wahhābism, of the Qāḍīzādelis in Ottoman

---

1 See in particular LAOUST, *Essai sur les doctrines sociales et politiques d'Ibn Taymīya* (1939), 525–30; SFEIR *& al.*, *Dictionnaire mondial de l'islamisme* (2002), 480; BENJAMIN & SIMON, *The Age of Sacred Terror* (2002), 52–53; ZEIDAN, 'The Islamic Fundamentalist View of Life as a Perennial Battle' (2001), 40; JANSEN, *De radicaal-islamitische ideologie*, 9.

2 See LAOUST, *Essai sur les doctrines*, 475–575; 'L'influence d'Ibn Taymiyya' (1979); MICHEL, 'Ibn Taymiyya: Islamic Reformer' (1985), 227–32; NAFI, 'Abu al-Thanaʾ al-Alusi: an Alim, Ottoman Mufti, and Exegete of the Qurʾan' (2002), 466–67; '*Taṣawwuf* and Reform in Pre-Modern Islamic Culture: in Search of Ibrāhīm al-Kūrānī' (2002).

Turkey of the eleventh/seventeenth century?[1] It was out of the question to take on such an archaeology in this study. That said, I shall be henceforth on the lookout for every citation and (proper or improper) use of, every allusion and appeal to, the Mardin fatwa, as also to the anti-Mongol fatwas, of the Shaykh al-Islām, in post-Taymiyyan Muslim writing, and indeed most grateful to whoever would kindly point me to the same.

This work jumps abruptly across six centuries to juxtapose the infidelities, betrayals and incompetencies of too many activists and contemporary authors who appeal or lay claim to the ideas of Ibn Taymiyya. Even so, it should in theory enable a more correct appreciation of the Damascene Shaykh al-Islām and of his thought, at least among the fair-minded. However, I do not entertain many illusions on this score: indolence, ignorance and prejudice (among academics as much as among ideologues and activists of every hue) have their own momentum and mechanism.

Still, having myself been in the past the target, *urbi et orbi*, of a cabal of sanctimonious hypocrites, I can believe this to be a work of a nature that might, all the same, lead to my 'rehabilitation'. 'At any rate,' a friend wrote to me, 'you should

---

1 On Qāḍīzāde Meḥmed b. Muṣṭafā (d. 1045/1635) and his reformist movement, see M. C. ZILFI, 'The Kadizadelis: Discordant Revivalism in Seventeenth Century Istanbul' (1986); *The Politics of Piety: The Ottoman Ulema in the Postclassical Age, 1600-1800* (1988), 129–81. On the influence of Ibn Taymiyya on Qāḍīzāde Meḥmed, see S. Çavuşoğlu, art. 'Kadizâdeliler', *İSLĀM ANSİKLOPEDİSİ* (1988—), xxiv. 100.

become politically correct again in the eyes of your enemies. But, as those remain people of bad faith, you should not expect too much by way of objective reactions.' May I then look forward to being treated as a 'bearded one' who (in the idiom of counter-terrorism) has been 'turned'…? But God is more knowing of the essence of hearts and He takes on the defence of those who believe.

Finally, my thanks to all those without whom this work would not have been. First of all, a wonderful colleague, the learned signatory of the Foreword, Professor James Piscatori, in the office next to my own: by him the aptness of the famous Arab proverb is once more wholly confirmed: *al-jār qabla l-dār.* I think next of the brothers and friends with whom I have discussed this book or who agreed to read drafts of it and let me share their comments and advice: Shahab Ahmed, Dimitris Antoniou, Salah Basalamah, François Burgat, Emran Islam, Jamil Qureshi. I have also benefited greatly from audience questions following presentations of my research on this subject, during the winter of 2003/2004, at the invitation of the Présence Musulmane society in Montreal, the Association des Étudiant(e)s Musulman(e)s of Laval University in Québec, the Centre for Middle Eastern and Islamic Studies in Cambridge, and the Institut Supérieur Islamique (Mosquée al-Khalīl) in Brussels. My sincere thanks to the organizers of these presentations.

L., A., and Kh. deserve actions rather than words.

This work is humbly dedicated to the memory of the many – may the compassion of God shelter them – martyred by the Mongols of our time and their flunkies.

Yahya Michot
Oxford, 22 March 2004

BIBLIOGRAPHY

(In alpha-sorting the entries in this list, the article *al-* and the consonant *ᶜayn* (shown as ᶜ) are ignored; the accentuated consonants ḍ, ḥ, ṣ, ṭ, ẓ are placed like their unaccentuated equivalents. Internet addresses appear within angle brackets: any spaces showing within those brackets should be ignored.)

ABOU EL FADL, K., *Rebellion and Violence in Islamic Law*. Cambridge: Cambridge University Press, 2001.

ABŪ DĀʾŪD (d. 275/889), *al-Sunan*. Ed. M. M. D. ᶜAbd al-Ḥamīd. 4 vols. Beirut: Dār al-Fikr, n.d.

ABŪ L-FIDĀʾ, Ismāᶜīl (d. 732/1331), *Kitāb Taqwīm al-buldān – Géographie*. Eds. M. Reinaud and MacGuckin de Slane. Paris: Imprimerie royale, 1840.

—, *al-Mukhtaṣar fī akhbār al-bashar*. 4 vols. Cairo: Maktabat al-Mutanabbī, n. d.

AḤMED, R. S., *al-Nabī al-musallaḥ, I: al-Rāfiḍūn – The Militant Prophet, I: The Rejectionists*. London: Riad el-Rayyes Books, 1991.

ᶜĀlam. = *Mawsūᶜat al-Ḥadīth al-Sharīf* (CD-ROM), 1st edn. Kuwait: Ṣakhr ᶜĀlamiyya, 1995.

ALLOUCHE, A., 'A Study of Ibn Baṭṭūṭah's Account of His 726/1326 Journey through Syria and Arabia', *Journal of Semitic Studies*, 36 (1990; Oxford), 283–99.

AMITAI-PREISS, R., 'Ghāzān, Islām, and Mongol Tradition: A View from the Mamlūk Sultanate', *Bulletin of the School of Oriental and African Studies*, 59 (1996), 1–10.

—, 'Mongol Imperial Ideology and the Ilkhanid War against the Mamluks', in R. Amitai-Preiss & D. O. Morgan (eds.), *The Mongol Empire and its Legacy*. Leiden: Brill, 'Islamic History & Civilization. Studies & Texts, 24', 1999, 57–72.

Anonymous, 'Le Wahhabisme', in *The Europ@sian News*, 99 (25 Sept. 2001). Internet: <*www.europasia.org/99.html*>.

al-Aqṣaraʾī, Muḥammad (d. 749/1348), *Nihāyat al-suʾl wa-l-umniyya fī ʿilm al-furūsiyya*. London, MS *BL Add 18866*.

Autonomie, *Pendant les attentats, le bourrage de crâne continue.* Communiqué du 09.11.2001. Internet: <*www.autonomie.org./messages/011109.htm*>.

Aydin, S., K. Emiroğlu, O. Özel, S. Ünsal, *Mardin: Aşiret, Cemaat, Devlet.* Istanbul: Türkiye Ekonomik ve Toplumsal Tarih Vakfı, 2000.

al-ʿAynī, Badr al-Dīn Muḥammad (d. 855/1451), *ʿIqd al-jumān fī taʾrīkh ahl al-zamān. ʿAṣr salāṭīn al-Mamālīk. (3) Ḥawādith wa tarājim 689–697h./1290–1298m.* Ed. M. M. Amīn. Cairo: G.E.B.O., 1410/1990.

ʿAzzām, ʿAbd Allāh, *Iʿlān al-jihād.* (?1988). Internet: <*www.geocities.com/ebadteam/images/algehad/e3lanalgehad.htm*>.

Başgelen, N., *Bir zamanlar Mardin.* Istanbul: Kentbank, 2000.

Bashier, Z., *Hijra: Story and Significance.* Leicester: The Islamic Foundation, 1403/1983.

Benjamin, D. & S. Simon, *The Age of Sacred Terror.* New York: Random House, 2002.

Bori, C., *Ibn Taymiyya: una vita esemplare. Analisi delle fonti classiche della sua biografia.* Rome–Pisa: Istituti editoriali e poligrafici internazionali, 'Supplemento no. 1 alla *Rivista degli Studi Orientali*, vol. LXXVI', 2003.

BOSWORTH, C. E., *The Mediaeval Islamic Underworld. The Banū Sāsān in Arabic Society and Literature.* 2 vols. Leiden: Brill, 1976.

—, *New Islamic Dynasties.* Edinburgh: Edinburgh University Press, 2004. (Revised, enlarged edition of *Islamic Dynasties*, 1967 [repr. 1980].)

BREYDENBACH (VON), Bernhard (d. 1497), *Peregrinatio in Terram Sanctam.* Saragossa: P. Hurus, 1498.

BUCKINGHAM, J. S., *Travels in Mesopotamia, including a Journey from Aleppo, across the Euphrates to Orfah....* 2 vols. London: Henry Colburn, 1827.

AL-BUKHĀRĪ, Muḥammad (d. 256/870), *al-Ṣaḥīḥ.* 9 vols. Bulaq: al-Maṭbaᶜat al-Kubrā l-Amīriyya, 1311–13 [1893–95].

BUNT, G., *Virtually Islamic: Computer-mediated Communication and Cyber Islamic Environments.* Cardiff: University of Wales Press, 'Religion, Culture and Society', 2000.

CARRÉ, O., *Mystique et politique: Lecture révolutionnaire du Coran par Sayyid Quṭb, Frère musulman radical.* Paris: Le Cerf – Presses de la Fondation Nationale des Sciences Politiques, 'Patrimoines. Islam', 1984.

CHARLES-DOMINIQUE, P., *Voyageurs arabes: Ibn Faḍlān, Ibn Jubayr, Ibn Baṭṭūṭa et un auteur anonyme.* Translated texts with introduction and notes. Paris: Gallimard, 'Nrf', 1995.

COOK, M., *Commanding Right and Forbidding Wrong in Islamic Thought.* Cambridge: Cambridge University Press, 2000.

DAGHER, J. & G. TROUPEAU, *Ibn Buṭlān. Le banquet des prêtres. Une* maqāma *chrétienne du XIe siècle.* Paris: Geuthner, 2004.

AL-DĀRIMĪ, Abū Muḥammad ᶜAbd Allāh (d. 255/869), *al-Sunan.* 2 vols. Cairo: Dār al-Fikr, 1398/1978. (Repr. Beirut: Dār al-Fikr, n. d.)

DELONG-BAS, N. J., *Wahhabi Islam: From Revival and Reform to Global Jihad.* London: I. B. Tauris, 2004.

DEWEY, W. C. (Rev.), 'Mardin in Mesopotamia', *The Missionary Herald: Containing the Proceedings of the American Board of Commissioners for Foreign Missions, with a View of Other Benevolent Operations for the Year 1889*, 85 (Boston: Samuel Usher, 1889), 94–97.

DOLAPÖNÜ, H., *Tarihte Mardin: İtr-el-nardin fi tarih Merdin.* Istanbul: Hilal Matbaacılık, 1972.

EI^2 = *Encyclopaedia of Islam*, 2nd edn. Leiden: E. J. Brill. Vol. 1, 1960; vols. 2–10, Supplement, 1965–2002.

FANDY, M., *Saudi Arabia and the Politics of Dissent.* London: Macmillan, 1999.

FARAJ, ʿAbd al-Salām, *al-Farīḍat al-ghāʾiba.* Cairo, 1981. Internet: <*www.alkalema.us/algehad/*>. (See also: AḤMED, *al-Nabī al-musallaḥ*, *I*, 127–49; ZAQZŪQ (ed.), *al-Fatāwā*, 3761–91; JANSEN, *The Neglected Duty*.)

GABRIEL, A., *Voyages archéologiques dans la Turquie Orientale*, with a collection of Arabic inscriptions by J. Sauvaget. 2 vols. Paris: Éditions de Boccard, 1940.

GIBB, H. A. R., *The Travels of Ibn Baṭṭūta, AD 1325–1354. Translated with revisions and notes from the Arabic text edited by C. Defrémery & B. R. Sanguinetti.* 5 vols. London: Hakluyt Society; Syndics of the Cambridge University Press. Vol. 2, 1956.

GUEST, J., *The Yezidis: A Study in Survival, Mesopotamia, Chaldea and Armenia.* London, n.d.

GUO, L., *Early Mamlūk Syrian Historiography: al-Yūnīnī's Dhayl Mirʾāt al-zamān.* 2 vols. Leiden: E. J. Brill, 'Islamic History and Civilization. Studies and Texts, 21', 1998.

HALEVI, J. D., 'al-Qaeda's Intellectual Legacy: New Radical Islamic Thinking Justifying the Genocide of Infidels', *Jerusalem Viewpoints*, 508 (1 Dec. 2003). Internet: <*www.jcpa.org/jl/vp508.htm*>.

ḤĀMIDULLĀH, M., *al-Shaybānī: Le grand livre de la conduite de l'État*. With the commentary of Abū Bakr al-Sarakhsī (d. 483/1090). Translated from the Hyderabad–Deccan and Cairo editions, as well as various MSS in Paris, Beirut and Istanbul. 4 vols. Ankara: Türkiye Diyanet Vakfı, 1989.

HAYKEL, B., 'Radical Salafism: Osama's Ideology', *Dawn* (2001). Internet: <*muslim-canada.org/binladendawn.html*>.

IBN ᶜABD AL-HĀDĪ, Abū ᶜAbd Allāh (d. 744/1343), *al-ᶜUqūd al-durriyya min manāqib shaykh al-islām Aḥmad bin Taymiyya*. Ed. M. Ḥ. al-Fiqī. Cairo: Maṭbaᶜat Ḥijāzī, 1357/1938.

IBN ABĪ YAᶜLĀ (d. 526/1132), *Ṭabaqāt al-Ḥanābila*. Eds. A. Ḥ. b. Ḥasan and A. Z. Bahjat. 4 vols. Beirut: Dār al-Kutub al-ᶜIlmiyya, 1417/1997.

IBN BAṬṬŪṬA (d. 779/1378?), *Riḥla*. See GIBB, CHARLES-DOMINIQUE.

IBN BUṬLĀN (d. 1066), *Maqāma*. See DAGHER & TROUPEAU.

IBN ḤANBAL (d. 241/855), *al-Musnad*. 6 vols. Cairo: al-Bābī l-Ḥalabī, 1313 [1896]. (Repr. Beirut: al-Maktab al-Islāmī, 1403/1983.)

IBN AL-JAZARĪ, Shams al-Dīn (d. 738/1337), *Taʾrīkh ḥawādith al-zamān wa-anbāʾi-hi wa-wafiyyāt al-akābir wa-l-aᶜyān min abnāʾi-hi*. Ed. ᶜU. ᶜA. S. Tadmurī. 3 vols. Sidon/Beirut: al-Maktabat al-ᶜAṣriyya, 1419/1998.

IBN KATHĪR (d. 774/1373), *al-Bidāya wa-l-nihāya*. Eds. A. Abū Mulḥim, F. al-Sayyid, ᶜA. N. ᶜAṭawī, M. Nāṣir al-Dīn, ᶜA. ᶜAbd al-Sātir. 14 parts in 8 vols. Cairo: Dār al-Rayyān li-l-Turāth, 1408/1988.

—, *Tafsīr al-Qurʾān al-ʿaẓīm*. 4 vols. Beirut: Dār al-Jayl, 1410/1990.

IBN MĀJA (d. 273/887), *al-Sunan*. Ed. M. F. ʿAbd al-Bāqī. 2 vols. Cairo, 1373/1954. (Repr. Beirut: Dār al-Fikr, n. d.)

IBN NAQĪB AL-MIṢRĪ, Aḥmad (d. 769/1368), *ʿUmdat al-sālik wa-ʿuddat al-nāsik*. See KELLER.

IBN QAYYIM AL-JAWZIYYA (d. 751/1350), *al-Ṭuruq al-ḥikmiyya fī l-siyāsat al-sharʿiyya*, aw *al-Firāsat al-murḍiya fī aḥkām al-siyāsat al-sharʿiyya*. Ed. S. ʿUmrān. Cairo: Dār al-Ḥadīth, 1423/2002.

IBN TAYMIYYA (d. 728/1328), *Majmūʿ al-fatāwā*. Ed. ʿA. R. b. M. Ibn Qāsim. 37 vols. Rabat: Maktabat al-Maʿārif, 1401/1981. [F].

CD-ROM *Majmūʿ fatāwā Ibn Taymiyya*. Cairo: Ḥarf Information Technology, 1999 (version 1.0).

See also MICHOT, *Ibn Taymiyya. Lettre à un roi croisé*; *Textes spirituels*.

—, *Darʾ taʿāruḍ al-ʿaql wa-l-naql*. Ed. M. R. Sālim. 11 vols. Riyadh: Dār al-Kunūz al-Adabiyya, 1399/1979.

—, *al-Istiqāma*. Ed. M. R. Sālim. 2 vols. Riyadh: Dār al-Faḍīla li-l-Nashr wa-l-Tawzīʿ; Beirut: Dār Ibn Ḥazm li-l-Ṭibāʿa wa-l-Nashr wa-l-Tawzīʿ, 1420/2000.

—, *al-Masāʾil al-Mārdīniyya*. Ed. M. Ḥ. al-Fiqī. Cairo: Maktabat al-Sunnat al-Muḥammadiyya, 1980.

—, *Minhāj al-sunnat al-nabawiyya fī naqḍ kalām al-Shīʿat al-qadariyya*. Ed. M. R. Sālim. 9 vols. Cairo: Maktabat Ibn Taymiyya, 1409/1989. [M].

—, *Kitāb al-Nubuwwāt*. Beirut: Dār al-Fikr, n.d.

—, *Qāʿida fī ziyāra Bayt al-Maqdis*. Ed. MATTHEWS, 'A Muslim Iconoclast', 1–21.

—, *al-Siyāsat al-sharʿiyya*. Ed. LAOUST, *Le traité de droit public d'Ibn Taymīya*, 45–194 Ar.

—, CD-ROM *Muʾallafāt al-shaykh wa-tilmīdhi-hi*. Amman: al-Turāth, 1420/1999 (version 1.0).

İSLĀM ANSİKLOPEDİSİ. Istanbul: Türkiye Diyanet Vakfı, 1988—

JACQUARD, R., *Au nom d'Oussama Ben Laden... Dossier secret sur le terroriste le plus recherché du monde*. Paris: Jean Picollec, 2001.

—, *Les archives secrètes d'al-Qaida. Révélations sur les héritiers de Ben Laden*. Paris: Jean Picollec, 2002.

JACKSON, S. A., 'Ibn Taymiyyah on Trial in Damascus', *Journal of Semitic Studies*, 39.1 (1994; Oxford), 41–85.

JĀD AL-ḤAQQ, J. Ḥ. ʿA., *Kutayb al-farīḍat al-ghāʾiba wa-l-radd ʿalay-hi*. Ed. in ZAQZŪQ, *al-Fatāwā*, vol. x, 3724–59, no. 1326.

JANSEN, J. J. G., *The Neglected Duty: The Creed of Sadat's Assassins and Islamic Resurgence in the Middle East*. New York: Macmillan, 1986.

—, 'Ibn Taymiyyah and the Thirteenth Century: a Formative Period of Modern Muslim Radicalism', *Quaderni di Studi Arabi*, 5–6 (1987–88). Atti del XIII Congresso dell'-Union Européenne d'Arabisants et d'Islamisants (Venice 29 Sept.–4 Oct. 1986). Venice: Armena, 391–96.

—, *De radicaal-islamitische ideologie: van Ibn Taymiyya tot Osama ben Laden*. (Speech, 3 February, 2004.) Utrecht: Universiteit Utrecht, Faculteit der Letteren, 2004.

AL-JARBŪʿ, ʿAbd al-ʿAzīz b. Ṣāliḥ, *Kitāb al-Iʿlām bi-wujūb al-hijra min dār al-kufr ilā dār al-islām*. 2001. <*www.khayma.com /wahbi/Research/Now/elam/main.htm*>.

KELLER, N. H. M. (ed. and trans.) *Reliance of the Traveller. The Classic Manual of Islamic Sacred Law,* ʿUmdat al-Sālik *by Aḥmad ibn Naqīb al-Miṣrī (d. 769/1368).* In Arabic with facing

English text, commentary, and appendices. Evanston, IL: Sunna Books, 1994.

KEPEL, G., *Le Prophète et Pharaon. Aux sources des mouvements islamistes.* Paris: Seuil, 'L'épreuve des faits', (revised and enlarged edition) 1993. (First edn: Paris: Éditions La Découverte, 1984. English trans.: *The Prophet & Pharaoh: Muslim Extremism in Egypt.* London: Al Saqi Books, 1985.)

—, *Jihad. Expansion et déclin de l'islamisme.* Paris: Gallimard, 2000.

— & Y. RICHARD, (eds.), *Intellectuels et militants de l'islam contemporain*, Paris: Seuil, 'Sociologie', 1990.

AL-KHALLĀL, Abū Bakr Aḥmad b. Muḥammad (d. 311/923), *al-Sunna.* Ed. ʿA. b. ʿA. al-Zahrānī. 5 parts in 2 vols. Riyadh: Dār al-Rāya, 1415/1994.
Manuscript: London, *BL Or. 2675.*

AL-KIBBĪ, Saʿd al-Dīn b. Muḥammad, *Tabṣīr al-ʿibād bi-taḥqīq baʿḍ masāʾil al-jihād.* Beirut, n.d. Internet: <*www.assiraj.biz land.com/library/jihad.htm*>.

LAOUST, H., *Essai sur les doctrines sociales et politiques de Taqī-d-Dīn Aḥmad b. Taymīya, canoniste ḥanbalite né à Ḥarrān en 661/1262, mort à Damas en 728/1328.* Cairo: I.F.A.O., 'Recherches d'archéologie, de philologie et d'histoire, IX', 1939.

—, 'La biographie d'Ibn Taymīya d'après Ibn Kathīr', *Bulletin d'Études Orientales*, 9 (1942–43) (Beirut: Institut Français de Damas, 1943), 115–62.

—, 'Le réformisme d'Ibn Taimīya', *Islamic Studies*, 1 (1962; Karachi: The Central Institute of Islamic Research), 27–47.

—, 'L'influence d'Ibn Taymiyya', in A. T. Welch & P. Cachia (eds.) *Islam: Past Influence and Present Challenge* (Edinburgh: Edinburgh University Press, 1979), 15–33.

—, *Le traité de droit public d'Ibn Taymīya*. Annotated trans. of *al-Siyāsat al-sharʿīya*. Re-edited with an introduction to the work by A. S. Djebbari. Algiers: 'El-Aniss', ENAG, 1990.

Lech, K., *Das mongolische Weltreich. Al-ʿUmarī's Darstellung der mongolischen Reiche in seinem Werk* Masālik al-abṣār wa-mamālik al-amṣār, *mit Paraphrase und Kommentar herausgegeben*. Wiesbaden: Otto Harrassowitz, 1968.

Little, D. P., 'Did Ibn Taymiyya Have a Screw Loose?', *Studia Islamica*, 41 (1975; Paris), 93–111.

—, 'Religion under the Mamluks', *The Muslim World*, 73 (July–Oct. 1983), 165–81.

Madelung, W., 'Has the Hijra come to an end?', *Revue des Études Islamiques* 54 (1986; Paris), 225–37.

al-Maghlūth, Ghāzī, 'Ibn Taymiyya…wa-fiqh al-qatl', *al-Waṭan*, 498 (26 Dhū l-Qaʿda 1422/9 Feb. 2002; Abha, Saudi Arabia). Internet: <*www.alwatan.com.sa/daily/2002-02-09/writers/writers13.htm*>.

al-Masʿarī, Muḥammad b. ʿAbd Allāh, *al-Adillat al-qaṭʿiyya ʿalā ʿadam sharʿiyyat al-dawlat al-saʿūdiyya*. London: Alharamain Islamic Information Center, 1418/1997. Internet: <*www.alhramain.com/text/kotob/5/f.htm*>.

Masud, M. K., 'The Obligation to Migrate: the Doctrine of *Hijra* in Islamic Law', in D. F. Eickelman & J. Piscatori (eds.), *Muslim Travellers: Pilgrimage, Migration, and the Religious Imagination*. Berkeley: University of California Press, 'Comparative Studies on Muslim Societies, 9', 1990.

Matthews, C. D., 'A Muslim Iconoclast (Ibn Taymiyyeh) on the "Merits" of Jerusalem and Palestine', *Journal of the American Oriental Society* 56 (1936; New Haven), 1–21.

MAWLAWI, F., *Dar al-Kufr: An Abode of Daʿwah, not War.* 2002. Internet: <*www.islamonline.net/fatwa/english/FatwaDisplay.asp?hFatwaID=72774*>.

MELVILLE, C., 'Pādishāh-i Islām: The Conversion of Ghāzān to Islām', *Pembroke Papers* 1 (1990), 159–77.

MICHEL, T. F., 'Ibn Taymiyya: Islamic Reformer', *Studia Missionalia*, 34: *Réformateurs religieux. Christianisme et les autres religions* (Rome: Gregorian University Press, 1985), 213–32.

MICHOT, Y. J., *Ibn Taymiyya. Lettre à Abū l-Fidā.* Translation from the Arabic, introduction, notes and glossary. Louvain-la-Neuve: Catholic University of Louvain, 1994.

—, *Ibn Taymiyya. Lettre à un roi croisé (al-Risālat al-Qubruṣiyya).* Translation from the Arabic, introduction, notes and glossary. Louvain-la-Neuve: Academia; Lyon: Tawhid, 'Sagesses musulmanes 2', 1995.

—, *Ibn Taymiyya. Les intermédiaires entre Dieu et l'homme.* French trans. of *Risālat al-wāsiṭa bayna l-khalq wa-l-ḥaqq*, followed by *Le Shaykh de l'Islam Ibn Taymiyya: chronique d'une vie de théologien militant.* Paris: A.E.I.F. Éditions, 'Fetwas du Shaykh de l'Islam Ibn Taymiyya, I', 1417/1996.

—, *Ibn Taymiyya. Le statut des moines.* French translation, with reference to the Tibéhirine affair, by Nasreddin Lebatelier (*Rubbān al-ghāriqīn fī qatl ruhbān Tībḥirīn*). Beirut: El-Safīna, 1417/1997.

—, 'Vanités intellectuelles… L'impasse des rationalismes selon *le Rejet de la contradiction* d'Ibn Taymiyya', *Oriente Moderno*, 19 n. s. (2000; Rome), 597–617.

—, 'Un célibataire endurci et sa maman: Ibn Taymiyya (d. 728/1328) et les femmes', in C. Cannuyer (ed.), *La femme dans les civilisations orientales.* Brussels: Société Belge d'Études Orientales, 'Acta Orientalia Belgica XV', 2001, 165–90.

—, *Ibn Taymiyya. Le Haschich et l'extase.* Texts trans. from the Arabic, with introduction and notes. Beirut: Albouraq, 'Fetwas d'Ibn Taymiyya III', 2001.

—, *Ibn Taymiyya. Un Dieu hésitant?* Text trans. from the Arabic, with introduction and notes. Beirut: Albouraq, 'Écrits spirituels d'Ibn Taymiyya I', 1425/2004.

—, 'Textes spirituels d'Ibn Taymiyya. VI: La foi et l'amour: du tawḥīd théorique à sa mise en oeuvre effective', *Le Musulman*, 19 (June–Sept. 1992; Paris: A.E.I.F.), 11–16.

—, 'Textes spirituels d'Ibn Taymiyya. VII: La servitude d'adoration, ou la perfection dans la liberté du coeur', *Le Musulman*, 20 (Sept. –Dec. 1992; Paris: A.E.I.F.), 10–15.

—, 'Textes spirituels d'Ibn Taymiyya. VIII: L'unité de la communauté (*umma*), dans la tolérance et la rigueur', *Le Musulman*, 21 (Dec. 1992–Mar. 1993; Paris: A.E.I.F.), 10–15.

—, 'Textes spirituels d'Ibn Taymiyya. X: "Je ne suis dans cette affaire qu'un musulman parmi d'autres… " ', *Le Musulman*, 23 (May 1994; Paris: A.E.I.F.), 27–32.

—,'Textes spirituels d'Ibn Taymiyya. XI: Mongols et Mamlūks: l'état du monde musulman vers 709/1310', *Le Musulman*, 24 (Oct. 1994; Paris, A.E.I.F.), 26–31.

—, 'Textes spirituels d'Ibn Taymiyya. XII: Mongols et Mamlūks: l'état du monde musulman vers 709/1310 (continuation)', *Le Musulman*, 25 (Jan. 1995; Paris, A.E.I.F.), 25–30.

—, 'Textes spirituels d'Ibn Taymiyya. XIII: Mongols et Mamlūks: l'état du monde musulman vers 709/1310 (conclusion)', *Le Musulman*, 26 (Sept. 1995; Paris, A.E.I.F.), 25–30.

—, 'Textes spirituels d'Ibn Taymiyya. XIV: Raison, confession, Loi: une typologie musulmane du religieux', *Le Musulman*, 27 (Jan. 1996; Paris: A.E.I.F.), 24–29.

—, 'Textes spirituels d'Ibn Taymiyya. XV: La réalité de l'amour (*maḥabba*) de Dieu et de l'homme', *Le Musulman*, 28 (Nov. 1996; Paris: A.E.I.F.), 24–27.

—, 'Textes spirituels d'Ibn Taymiyya. XVI: La réalité de l'amour (*maḥabba*) de Dieu et de l'homme (continuation)', *Le Musulman*, 29 (Muḥarr. 1418/May 1998; Paris: A.E.I.F.), 20–25.

(The 'Textes spirituels' can also be read on the internet at: <*www.muslimphilosophy.com/it/default.htm*>.)

—, 'Rashīd al-Dīn et Ibn Taymiyya: regards croisés sur la royauté', *Mohaghegh Nāma* (Collected papers presented to Professor Mehdi Mohaghegh on his 70th birthday in appreciation of his 50 years' academic activities. Supervised by B. Khorramshāhī and J. Jahānbakhsh). 2 vols. Tehran: Sinānegār, 2001. Vol. 2, 111–37.

—, 'A Mamlūk Theologian's Commentary on Avicenna's *Risāla Aḍḥawiyya*: Being a Translation of a Part of the *Darʾ al-taʿāruḍ* of Ibn Taymiyya, with Introduction, Annotation, and Appendices', Part I, *Journal of Islamic Studies*, 14.2 (May 2003; Oxford), 149–203; Part II, 14.3 (Sept. 2003), 309–63.

—, *Pour une tombe à Damas. Texte et photographies par Yahya Michot.* Internet: <*www.saphirnews.com/Pour-une-tombe,-a-Damas-4483.html*>

MILSON, M., 'Reform *vs.* Islamism in the Arab World Today', *Special Report* 34 (15 Sept. 2004). The Middle East Media Research Institute (MEMRI). Internet: <*memri.org/bin/articles.cgi?Page=archives&Area=sr&ID=SR3404*>.

MISIRLIOĞLU, İ. (ed.), *Mardin: Poetry of Stone and Faith*. Istanbul: The Economic and Social History Foundation of Turkey, 1998.

MONIQUET, C., *Le Djihad. Histoire secrète des hommes et des réseaux en Europe*. Paris: Ramsay, 'Documents', 2004.

MURAD, H. Q., 'Ibn Taymiyya on Trial: A Narrative Account of His *miḥan*', *Islamic Studies* 18 (1979; Islamabad: The Islamic Research Institute), 1–32.

MUSLIM (d. 261/875), *al-Jāmiᶜ al-ṣaḥīḥ*. 8 vols. Constantinople, 1334 [/1916]. (Repr. Beirut: al-Maktab al-Tijārī li-l-Ṭibāᶜa wa-l-Nashr wa-l-Tawzīᶜ, n.d.)

NAFI, B. M., 'Abu al-Thanaᵓ al-Alusi: an Alim, Ottoman Mufti, and Exegete of the Qurᵓan', *International Journal of Middle East Studies* 34 (2002), 465–94.

—, '*Taṣawwuf* and Reform in Pre-Modern Islamic Culture: in Search of Ibrāhīm al-Kūrānī', *Die Welt des Islams* 42.3 (2002; Leiden), 307–55.

AL-NASĀᵓĪ (d. 303/915), *al-Sunan*. 8 vols. Beirut: Dār al-Kutub al-ᶜIlmiyya, n.d.

NIEBUHR, C., *Voyage en Arabie et en d'autres Pays circonvoisins*. Trans. from German. 2 vols. Amsterdam: S. J. Baalde; Utrecht: B. Wild, 1780.

OEMIW = *The Oxford Encyclopedia of the Modern Islamic World*, ed. J. L. Esposito. 4 vols. Oxford, 1995.

PARRY, O. H., *Six Months in a Syrian Monastery, Being the Record of a Visit to the Head Quarters of the Syrian Church in Mesopotamia, with Some Account of the Yazidis or Devil Worshippers of Mosul and el Jilwah, their Sacred Book*. Illustrated by the Author. London: Horace Cox, 1895.

PAZ, R., '*Qaedat al-jihad*: New Name on the Road to Palestine', *Policywatch* 623 (6 May, 2002). Internet: <*www.washingtoninstitute.org/watch/policywatch/policywatch2002/623.htm*>

RAMADAN, T., *Être Musulman Européen. Étude des sources islamiques à la lumière du contexte européen*. Lyon: Tawhid, 1999.

—, *Dār ash-shahāda: l'Occident, espace du témoignage*. Lyon: Tawhid, 'Questions contemporaines 4', 2002.

—, *Les Musulmans d'Occident et l'avenir de l'islam*. Arles: Actes Sud, 'Sindbad, L' Actuel', 2003.

RAPOPORT, Y. *Marriage, Money and Divorce in Medieval Islamic Society*. Cambridge: Cambridge University Press, 'Cambridge Studies in Islamic Civilization', 2005.

RASHĪD AL-DĪN, Faḍl Allāh (d. 718/1318), *Jāmiᶜ al-tawārīkh*. Eds. M. Rūshan & M. Mūsāwī. 4 vols. Tehran: Nashr-i Alburz, 1373 [/1994].

REX SMITH, C., *Medieval Muslim Horsemanship. A Fourteenth-Century Arabic Cavalry Manual*. London: The British Library, 1979.

SĀLIM, Zuhayr, *Waqfāt fī fiqh al-jihād*. London. Internet: <*www.asharq alarabi.org.uk/center1/dirasatjehad.htm*>.

SAQR, ᶜA., *Concept of Dar Al-Islam and Dar Al-Harb*, 2002. Internet: <*www.islamonline.net/fatwa/english/FatwaDisplay.asp?hFatwaID=51640*>.

SCHIMMEL, A., 'Some Glimpses of the Religious Life in Egypt during the Later Mamlūk Period', *Islamic Studies*, 4 (1965), 353–92.

SEVİM, M., *Gravürlerle Türkiye in Gravures, V: Anadolu – Anatolia, 2*. Ankara: T. C. Kültür Bakanlığı, 'Publications 1900. Works of Arts Series 125', 2002.

SFEIR, A. (ed.), *Dictionnaire mondial de l'islamisme*. Paris: Plon, 2002.

AL-SHAYBĀNĪ, Muḥammad b. al-Ḥasan (d. 189/805), *Kitāb al-siyar al-kabīr*. See ḤĀMIDULLĀH.

SHUMAYSĀNĪ, Ḥ, *Madīnat Mārdīn min al-fatḥ al-ʿarabī ilā sanat 921/1515*. Beirut: ʿĀlam al-Kitāb, 1407/1987.

SIVAN, E., 'Ibn Taymiyya: Father of the Islamic Revolution. Medieval Theology & Modern Politics', *Encounter*, 60.5 (1983), 41–50.

—, *Radical Islam. Medieval Theology and Modern Politics*. New Haven: Yale University Press, (enlarged edn.) 1990.

SORMAN, G., *Les enfants de Rifaa: musulmans et modernes*. Paris: Fayard, 2003.

—, *The Children of Rifaa: In Search of a Moderate Islam*. Trans. from French by Asha Puri. New Delhi: Penguin Books India, 'The French Collection', 2004.

TABBAA, Y., 'The Medieval Islamic Garden: Typology and Hydraulics', in J. D. Hunt (ed.), *Garden History: Issues, Approaches, Methods*. Washington: Dumbarton Oaks Research Library and Collection, 1992, 303–29.

TEITELBAUM, J., *Holier than Thou. Saudi Arabia's Islamic Opposition*. Washington: The Washington Institute for Near East Policy, 'Policy Papers 52', 2000.

AL-TIRMIDHĪ, Abū ʿĪsā (d. 279/893), *al-Sunan*. Ed. ʿA. R. M. ʿUthmān. 5 vols. Beirut: Dār al-Fikr, 2nd edn., 1403/1983.

AL-ʿUMARĪ, Shihāb al-Dīn (d. 749/1349), *Kitāb masālik al-abṣār wa-mamālik al-amṣār*. See LECH.

WEBSTER, R., '*Hijra* and the Dissemination of Wahhābī Doctrine in Saudi Arabia', in I. R. Netton (ed.), *Golden Roads: Migration, Pilgrimage and Travel in Mediaeval and Modern Islam*. Richmond: Curzon Press, 1993.

YĀQŪT (d. 626/1229), *Muʿjam al-buldān*. Ed. F. ʿA. ʿA. al-Jundī. 7 vols. Beirut: Dār al-Kutub al-ʿIlmiyya, 1410/1990.

YĀZĪJĪ ZĀDEH, Meḥmed (d. 855/1451), *Kitāb al-Muḥammadiyya fī l-kamālāt al-Aḥmadiyya*. Istanbul, 1284/1867.

AL-YŪNĪNĪ, Quṭb al-Dīn (d. 726/1326), *Dhayl Mirʾāt al-zamān*. See GUO.

ZAQZŪQ, M. Ḥ. (ed.), *al-Fatāwā l-Islāmiyya min Dār al-Iftāʾ al-Miṣriyya*, 21 vols. Cairo: Ministry of Waqfs, (2nd edn.) 1418/1997.

ZEIDAN, D., 'The Islamic Fundamentalist View of Life as a Perennial Battle', *Middle East Review of International Affairs* 5.4 (2001), 26–53.

ZILFI, M. C., 'The Kadizadelis: Discordant Revivalism in the Seventeenth Century Istanbul', *Journal of Near Eastern Studies*, 45 (1986), 251–69.

—, *The Politics of Piety: The Ottoman Ulema in the Postclassical Age (1600–1800)*. Minneapolis: Bibliotheca Islamica, 1988.

ZORZI, G. D., *La vera descritione de la gran cita del Caiero*. Venice: Matteo Pagano, *c.* 1546–1549.

Monastery of Dayr al-Zaʿfarān, near Mardin
Drawing by O. H. PARRY, *Six Months in a Syrian Monastery* (1895), frontispiece.

Appendix

SHAYKH AL-ISLĀM IBN TAYMIYYA

Chronology of the Life of an Activist–Theologian

For this summary overview of the life of the Shaykh al-Islām, I have relied on the works of the great Ibn Taymiyya scholar, Henri LAOUST (see Bibliography, above p. 140). However, these works, while they remain invaluable and I am very much indebted to them, were written half a century ago and need to be supplemented, at times corrected, in the light of subsequent scholarship. I have added various historical or bibliographical facts and corrected the dating of them. I have also drawn information from the excellent articles of Hasan Q. MURAD and Sherman JACKSON (above, pp. 145, 139) and, where relevant, included it in this Chronology. A recent work by Caterina BORI (*Ibn Taymiyya: una vita esemplare*, above p. 134) opens up new perspectives. I must record, nevertheless, that a full and sufficient biographical study of the Shaykh al-Islām, as well as an accurate dating of his prolific writing remain tasks as yet unaccomplished.

That said, the events recorded here, albeit skeletally, suffice to demonstrate that Ibn Taymiyya was true to the responsibilities, as he understood them, of an Islamic scholar, and true to the values he preached. In his own words (cited from p. 54 above): '*three fundamentals combin[e] everything:*

- *to obey within obedience to God, even if the one giving the order is unjust;*
- *to abstain from disputing the authority of those who dispose it;*
- *to take up the cause of the Truth without fear of any creature.*'

656/1258:

Destruction of Baghdād by the Mongols of Hūlāgū.

658/1260:

Victory of the Mamlūks over the Mongols at ʿAyn Jālūt. Assassination of the sultan Quṭuz and enthronement of the Turkish emir Rukn al-Dīn Baybars.

661/1263, 10 Rabīʿ I/22 January:

Birth of Taqī al-Dīn Aḥmad b. ʿAbd al-Ḥalīm b. ʿAbd al-Salām b. Taymiyya at Ḥarrān (Urfa), to a family of Ḥanbalī ulema.

663/1265:

Birth of Zayn al-Dīn ʿAbd al-Raḥmān, brother of Ibn Taymiyya. (Became a merchant trader; died in 747/1347.)

666/1268:

Birth of Sharaf al-Dīn ʿAbd Allāh, brother of Ibn Taymiyya. (Became a renowned scholar, highly esteemed by his brother, whose troubles he so often shared.)

667/1269:

Fleeing the Mongol threat, the family of Ibn Taymiyya take refuge in Damascus and settle there. His first teacher is his father. He then receives madrasa training – Qurʾān, ḥadīth, *fiqh*, Arabic language – from various shaykhs of the Ḥanbalī madrasas in Damascus. He studies in addition: *kalām* (theology), Sufism, logic, philosophy, and heresiography, notably Khārijism and Shīʿism.

676/1277:

Death in Damascus of the sultan Rukn al-Dīn Baybars.

678/1279:

Following the short-lived reigns of two of the children of Rukn al-Dīn Baybars, the enthronement as sultan of the Turkish emir, Qalāwūn.

678/1279–80:

At seventeen years old, Ibn Taymiyya is already considered qualified to give fatwas.

682/1283:

Death of Shaykh Ibn Abī ʿUmar b. Qudāma, first of two names in the *silsila* (the initiatic chain) through which Ibn Taymiyya – according to some classical sources, if not a statement of his own – links himself back to the great

Ḥanbalī Sufi shaykh, ʿAbd al-Qādir al-Gilānī of Baghdād (d. 561/1166).

683/1284, 2 Muḥarram/21 March:

Inaugural teaching session by Ibn Taymiyya, in the capacity of *shaykh al-ḥadīth*, at Dār al-Ḥadīth al-Sukariyya in Damascus, as the head of which he succeeds his father, who has just died. He makes an excellent impression.

684/1285, 10 Ṣafar/17 April:

Ibn Taymiyya begins the teaching of Qurʾānic exegesis at the Umayyad Mosque after the Friday prayer. A chair has been especially assigned to him.

689/1290, Dhū l-Qaʿda/November:

Death of Qalāwūn. Enthronement of his son, Khalīl.

690/1291:

Fall of Acre. End of the Crusades.

690/1291:

For certain of his statements about the attributes of God, at a teaching-session in the Umayyad Mosque some of the audience attack Ibn Taymiyya – they do so in vain.

691/1292, 7 Ṣafar/29 January:

Birth in Damascus of Ibn Qayyim al-Jawziyya, who will be the foremost disciple of Ibn Taymiyya.

691 end/1292 end:

Pilgrimage to Makka. Composition of *Manāsik al-ḥajj* ('The rites of the pilgrimage').

693/1293, Muḥarram/December:

Assassination of the sultan Khalīl by the sultan's deputy, Baydarā, who reigns only a few days before being killed. Beginning of the first reign of al-Nāṣir Muḥammad, aged eight, another son of Qalāwūn.

693/1294:

Public intervention by Ibn Taymiyya against a Christian clerk accused of having insulted the Prophet. Ibn Taymiyya suffers the bastinado and is kept under watch for a time, while the Christian converts. He composes on the subject his *Kitāb al-Ṣārim al-maslūl ʿalā shātim al-Rasūl* ('Book of the sword unsheathed against whoever insults the Messenger').

694/1294, Muḥarram/December:

Dismissal of al-Nāṣir and usurpation of the throne by the deputy-sultan Kitbugha l-Manṣūrī.

694/1295:

Conversion of the īlkhān Ghāzān, Mongol sovereign of Persia, to Sunnī Islam.

694/1295, 17 Ramaḍān/31 July:

Death of the Shāfiʿī shaykh, Sharaf al-Dīn Aḥmad al-Maqdisī, who took pride in and rejoiced at having authorized Ibn Taymiyya to give fatwas.

695/1296, 17 Shaʿbān/20 June:

Inaugural course by Ibn Taymiyya at Dār al-Ḥadīth al-Ḥanbaliyya, the oldest and most prestigious madrasa in Damascus, where he succeeds his teacher Zayn al-Dīn b. al-Munajjā, who passed away on 4 Shaʿbān/7 June.

696/1296, Muḥarram/November:

Kitbugha l-Manṣūrī is deposed by the Turkish emir, Lājīn, who exiles al-Nāṣir to al-Karak (Jordan) in Ṣafar 697/1298.

697/1298, 17 Shawwāl/27 July:

At the Umayyad Mosque Ibn Taymiyya holds a session of exhortation to jihād, in the context of military operations by the sultan Lājīn against the kingdom of Little Armenia, ally of the Tatars. These operations will fail and several emirs will go over to the Mongol camp, among them the governor of Damascus, Sayf al-Dīn Qibjaq.

698/1298, Rabīʿ I/December:

Ibn Taymiyya has composed his *al-ʿAqīdat al-ḥamawiyyat al-kubrā* ('The great creed of Ḥamāt') at the request of the people of Ḥamāt. Accused of assimilationism in his conception of the attributes of God, he refuses to appear before the council of the Ḥanafī qāḍī, Jalāl al-Dīn, whom he judges incompetent in questions of dogma and who has his fatwa publicly denounced. The provisional governor, Sayf al-Dīn Jāghān, sides with Ibn Taymiyya, of whom he is a faithful supporter, and subjects the public denouncer and his companions to the bastinado.

It is also with the support of Jāghān that Ibn Taymiyya is able to conduct his attacks on astrologers. His fatwas against astrology are most likely to be dated to this period. (Trans. in MICHOT, 'A Mamlūk Theologian's Commentary'; see also C. BORI, *Ibn Taymiyya: una vita esemplare*, 133–34.)

698/1298, 14 Rabīᶜ I/20 December:

Ibn Taymiyya of his own accord appears before the council of the Shāfiᶜī chief qāḍī, Imām al-Dīn, in order to discuss his *al-ᶜAqīdat al-ḥamawiyyat al-kubrā*, explains the passages of it that have been problematic, convinces his hearers, and is otherwise not further troubled.

Mamlūk and Mongol dominions

698/1298–99:

In this same year, he composes his *al-ᶜAqīdat al-Wāsiṭiyya* ('The creed of Wāsiṭ') for a Shāfiᶜī qāḍī of this town. At the time of his troubles in 705/1306 he will state that he wrote it 'some seven years ago, before the arrival of the Tatars in Syria' (*Majmūᶜ al-fatāwā*, iii. 163, 194, 203).

698/1299, Rabīᶜ II/January:

Following the assassination of Lājīn, the beginning of the second reign of al-Nāṣir, under the tutelage of the emirs, Baybars al-Jāshnikīr, a Circassian, and Salār, a Mongol.

699/1299–1300, Rabīᶜ I–Shaᶜbān/December–May:

First invasion of Syria by the īlkhān Ghāzān. After the defeat of the sultan al-Nāṣir at Wādī l-Khazindār, Ibn Taymiyya inspires the resistance of Damascus against the Tatar invader and his auxiliaries – Armenians, Georgians, and Cypriot Crusaders. Meeting the īlkhān, his vizier Rashīd al-Dīn Faḍl-Allāh (d. 718/1318) and other Mongol authorities, he obtains the release of Muslim, Christian and Jewish prisoners. (See MICHOT, *Lettre à un roi croisé.*)

699/1300, end Rajab/beginning April:

The Mongols having quit Damascus and the authority of the sultan re-established there, Ibn Taymiyya and his companions lead an anti-debauchery campaign in the brothels and taverns.

699/1300, Shawwāl–Dhū l-Ḥijja/summer:

Ibn Taymiyya takes part in an expedition against the Shīᶜa of the Syrian–Lebanese mountains, collaborators of the Tatars and the Crusaders from Cyprus.

700/1300–01, Ṣafar–Jumāda II/October–February:

Second attempted invasion of Syria by Ghāzān. Ibn Taymiyya exhorts the people and the army to the jihād, then heads to Cairo to appeal for the intervention of al-Nāṣir. He expounds to him the risks of Syria seceding if he does not mobilize to defend it.

After having plundered northern Syria with their allies – Armenians and Crusaders from Cyprus – the Tatars abandon their plans and cross back over the Euphrates.

700/1301, Jumāda II/March:

Some decisions are taken actually to apply to the dhimmīs of the Mamlūk sultanate the measures of the Sharīʿa pertaining to them.

701/1302, Shawwāl/June:

Ibn Taymiyya plays an active role in the inquiry into, and the rejection of, the demand for exemption from the poll-tax – the exemption having been introduced in Damascus by some Jews claiming descent from the former Jewish settlers of Khaybar expelled by the Prophet.

Several Jews of Damascus convert to Islam in this period – on occasion under the influence of Ibn Taymiyya, as is the case with the physician Ibn al-Muhadhdhib (d. 715/1315).

Some jealous persons accuse Ibn Taymiyya of himself carrying out the sanctions and penalties of the Law, as also of shaving the heads of children. He confounds these detractors.

702/1302, Ṣafar/September:

The Mamlūks capture from the Templars the island of Ruwād, the last Crusader stronghold in the East.

702/1302, Rabīʿ II/December:

Ibn Taymiyya is accused, in an anonymous letter addressed to al-Afram, the governor of Damascus, of maintaining relations with the Tatars and plotting a coup d'état in Syria. The official inquiry discovers the authors of the calumny and completely exonerates Ibn Taymiyya.

702/1303, Rajab–Ramaḍān/February–April:

Third invasion of Syria by the īlkhān Ghāzān. Ibn Taymiyya exhorts the army and fights with his disciples at the battle of Shaqḥab, which sees the victory of the sultan al-Nāṣir. In a fatwa he exempts the combatants from the fast. On his return to Damascus he receives the most enthusiastic welcome.

703/1304:

Ibn Taymiyya sends his *al-Risālat al-qubruṣiyya* ('The Cypriot Epistle') to Johan of Giblet, a Crusader king taking refuge in Cyprus, to ask him to release his Muslim prisoners or, at the least, to treat them well and to refrain from converting them to Christianity. (See MICHOT, *Lettre à un roi croisé*.)

703/1304, 4 Shawwāl/10 May:

Death of Ghāzān, and enthronement of his brother Öljāytū as īlkhān of Persia.

704/1305, Rajab/January:

Ibn Taymiyya criticizes the deviant shaykhs Mujāhid Ibrāhīm al-Qaṭṭān and Muḥammad al-Khabbāz. He obliges them to adopt a garb in keeping with the *Sunna* and make public acts of contrition.

He turns up at the mosque of al-Naranj in order to destroy there a 'sacred' rock, which had been made the object of various superstitions.

He also leads an epistolary campaign against the Sufi partisans of Ibn ʿArabī and the doctrine of the oneness of existence (*waḥdat al-wujūd*), among them in Cairo the shaykh Karīm al-Dīn al-Āmulī (d. 710/1310–11) and the shaykh Naṣr al-Dīn al-Manbijī (d. 719/1319), spiritual master of the powerful emir, Baybars al-Jāshnikīr.

704/1305, Dhū l-Ḥijja/June:

Expedition of Ibn Taymiyya and a group of his disciples against the Rāfiḍīs of Kasrawān, to alert them to the risks they court by persisting in their heresy and to impose on them the Law of Islam.

705/1305, 2 Muḥarram/25 July:

Another departure by Ibn Taymiyya into the Syrian–Lebanese mountains, in the context of a sizeable military operation that will cause much death and destruction.

705/1305, 9 Jumāda I/27 November:

Complaint by a group of Aḥmadiyya Sufis to the governor of Damascus, al-Afram, about the attacks against them by Ibn Taymiyya. In the course of a memorable public confrontation with the Shaykh al-Islām, their suit is dismissed, and their innovations, extravagances and wayward practices are condemned.

705/1306, 8, 12 Rajab/24, 28 January:

Set on by the intrigues of the shaykh Naṣr al-Dīn al-Manbijī, the sultan in a letter commands Ibn Taymiyya to explain himself before the governor of Damascus on the matter of his creed and some letters he may have sent to Egypt to urge adoption of that creed. Two councils are summoned for the purpose. Ibn Taymiyya produces his profession of faith, *al-Wāsitiyya*, explains it, and vehemently defends himself. On the subject of the attributes of God, the heart of the argument, he refuses to be considered a Ḥanbalī and claims to be adhering to the creed of the pious Ancients (*salaf*). At the end of the second council, both sides claim victory.

However, in the absence of the governor on a hunting expedition, and on instruction from authorities opposed to Ibn Taymiyya, several of his disciples are subjected to harassments.

Similarly, taking advantage of the governor's absence, the powerful Shāfiʿī chief qāḍī, Najm al-Dīn b. Ṣaṣrā (d. 723/1323), has the Shāfiʿī shaykh Jamāl al-Dīn al-Mizzī (d. 741/1341) imprisoned on an issue of dogma. Ibn Ṣaṣrā detests al-Mizzī all the more for being a friend of Ibn Taymiyya. The latter, without consulting any authority, goes in person to have al-Mizzī released and, upon the governor's return, complains to him.

705/1306, 7 Shaʿbān/21 February:

A third council is held, before the governor of Damascus, on the creed of Ibn Taymiyya (especially his conception of the attributes and the Word of God). Sundry doctors of the Law present become heated; Ibn Ṣaṣrā resigns, and Ibn Taymiyya is not condemned. The governor, apparently, sends a report to the sultan.

Ibn Taymiyya will present his own account of these three councils in a memoir written some years later. (It is translated in full by Sherman A. JACKSON, 'Ibn Taymiyya on Trial in Damascus' (1994), 56–85.)

705/1306, 26 Shaʿbān/21 March:
A letter of the sultan restores Ibn Ṣaṣrā to office and confirms the orthodoxy of Ibn Taymiyya.

705/1306, 5 Ramaḍān/21 March :
Another letter from the sultan severely denounces Ibn Taymiyya and summons him to Cairo, along with Ibn Ṣaṣrā and others. The sultan even re-opens the file on *al-ʿAqīdat al-ḥamawiyyat al-kubrā* (of 698/1298) and demands a copy of it, as also of *al-ʿAqīdat al-Wāsiṭiyya.* The governor of Damascus, learning that the case is being directly pursued by the emir Baybars al-Jāshnikīr, refuses to write to the sultan in order to help settle it.

705/1306, 22 Ramaḍān/7 April:
Ibn Taymiyya, his brothers Sharaf al-Dīn and Zayn al-Dīn (d. 747/1347), and Ibn Ṣaṣrā, arrive in Cairo. The next day, during the course of a council held in the citadel of Cairo before the emirs Salār and Baybars al-Jāshnikīr, the four chief qāḍīs of Egypt, and other dignitaries, Ibn Taymiyya is accused of assimilationism, notably on the subject of his conception of God's sitting on the Throne and His Word. The trial is iniquitous; the defendant is barely allowed to defend himself and, with his two brothers, is sentenced to prison by the ageing Mālikī chief qāḍī, Zayn al-Dīn ʿAlī b. Makhlūf (634–718/1236–1318), a disciple of Abū l-Ḥasan al-Shādhilī (d. 656/1258) and personal friend of shaykh Naṣr al-Dīn al-Manbijī, who detests Ibn Taymiyya.

705/1306, 26 Ramaḍān/11 April:
Beginning of the detention of Ibn Taymiyya and his two brothers Sharaf al-Dīn and Zayn al-Dīn in the citadel of Cairo. After some days of detention in one of the citadel's towers, where he was able to receive food and visits from emirs, he is sent down to the worst and lowest dungeon, 'the tank', on the order of the emir Baybars al-Jāshnikīr, at the urging of Ibn Makhlūf.

705/1306, 6 Dhū l-Qaʿda/20 May:
Returned to Damascus, Ibn Ṣaṣrā resumes his functions. At the Umayyad Mosque a letter of the sultan is read out justi-

fying the condemnation of Ibn Taymiyya and anathematizing his creed. This letter will subsequently be read out by public crier, and the Ḥanbalī disciples of Ibn Taymiyya compelled, before witnesses, to disown him. Identical persecutions will fall upon the Ḥanbalīs of Cairo.

706/1307, 30 Ramaḍān/4 April:

The emir Salār sets up a meeting of religious authorities to discuss the release of Ibn Taymiyya. Invited six times to appear, to correct his creed and to pledge not to present these questions of dogma before the people, Ibn Taymiyya refuses, and all but manhandles the emir al-Ṭaybarsī, who has been serving as go-between. (Extracts from two letters from prison, written by Ibn Taymiyya a little after these steps by Salār aimed at releasing him, are translated in MICHOT, 'Textes spirituels IX–X'. He speaks therein of the terrible conditions of his detention and of these efforts at conciliation that have remained without effect.)

706/1307, 27 Dhū l-Ḥijja/29 June:

Salār summons to his council the Mālikī qāḍī Ibn Makhlūf and the two brothers of Ibn Taymiyya imprisoned with him, Sharaf al-Dīn and Zayn al-Dīn, with a view to a conciliation. Sharaf al-Dīn defeats the qāḍī during the discussion. Ibn Taymiyya remains in prison.

706/1307, 28 Dhū l-Ḥijja/30 June:

On this Friday, the governor al-Afram gives a reading from a letter that Ibn Taymiyya has sent to him from his prison in Cairo, and eulogizes him.

707/1307, 14 Ṣafar/14 August:

At the citadel, Ibn Taymiyya has an interview with the chief Shāfiʿī qāḍī of Egypt, Badr al-Dīn b. Jamāʿa, but remains in prison.

707/1307, 23 Rabīʿ I/21 September:

At the initiative of the emir Salār and of a faithful supporter of Ibn Taymiyya, the Bedouin chief Ḥusām al-Dīn Muhannā b. ʿĪsā (d. 736/1335–36) – who, finding himself in Cairo at the time, has obtained from the sultan an authorization for release – Ibn Taymiyya agrees to come out of prison and to debate with various doctors of the Law before Salār. The qāḍīs decline the invitation.

707/1307, 25 Rabīᶜ I/23 September:

Ibn Taymiyya and his brothers are actually set free at the end of a second session of discussions, presided over by the emir Salār. However, Ibn Taymiyya is not authorized to return to Syria. After staying some days with Salār, he settles in the al-Ḥusayn quarter.

707/1307, 30 Rabīᶜ I/28 September:

On this Friday, after praying at al-Ḥākim mosque, Ibn Taymiyya declines the invitation extended to him to teach there. But then, being reminded of his religious–legal obligation to teach, he discharges that obligation and speaks till evening on worship and the appeal for help.

707/1307, 6 Rabīᶜ II/4 October:

A third council is held at the madrasa Ṣāliḥiyya, in which the qāḍīs also take part. Ibn Taymiyya is asked to go back over certain of his affirmations, and this time – unless this had already happened at one of the two preceding councils – he accepts certain amendments in the formulation of his creed.

Ibn Taymiyya then resumes public teaching in Cairo, and this is a very great success. He does not delay in criticizing Akbarī Sufism for the doctrine of the oneness of existence.

707/1308, Shawwāl/April:

Two Sufis, particularly influential in Egypt, the Shādhilī Ibn ᶜAṭāʾ Allāh (d. 709/1310) and Karīm al-Dīn al-Āmulī, have organized a noisy demonstration at the citadel in order to complain to the sultan and the emirs about Ibn Taymiyya's attacks against them and against the ideas of Ibn ᶜArabī. Ibn Taymiyya is summoned before the Shāfiᶜī chief qāḍī of Egypt, Badr al-Dīn b. Jamāᶜa, and interrogated about his conception of the intercession of the Prophet and about appeal for his help. However, no charge is retained against him, and he leaves this council more determined than ever.

With the complaints about him continuing, Ibn Taymiyya is finally called on to choose between prison and residing under surveillance in either Alexandria or Damascus. He chooses prison, but a group of his companions persuade him to return with them to Damascus.

707/1308, 19 Shawwāl/11 April:

The day after his departure for Damascus, Ibn Taymiyya is led back to Cairo at the instigation of Ibn Makhlūf. After a new council at the court of Badr al-Dīn b. Jamāᶜa, he himself, with the public interest (*maṣlaḥa*) in mind, turns himself over for imprisonment. Held in the prison of the qāḍīs, he obtains a sufficiently liberal regime to permit him to continue his activity. Notably, he calls the other prisoners back to their religious duties and, little by little, transforms the prison into a sort of *zāwiya*. His brother Zayn al-Dīn and various disciples are with him.

708/1309, Ramaḍān/February

Abandonment of the throne by al-Nāṣir, who takes refuge with his Mamlūks in al-Karak. The emir, Baybars al-Jāshnikīr, who is known to be not well-disposed toward Ibn Taymiyya, soon proclaims himself sultan.

Ibn Taymiyya does not hesitate to criticize the new regime, and considers as numbered the days of Baybars al-Jāshnikīr and of his spiritual master al-Manbijī.

709/1309–10, 30 Ṣafar–beg. Shawwāl /7–8 August–beg. March:

Baybars transfers Ibn Taymiyya, without his companions, to Alexandria and assigns a residence for him there. Ten days later in Damascus, rumour will have it that he was assassinated during the journey.

However, his companions are soon authorized to join him. He is allowed to receive visitors, to teach and to write, to go to the baths and to the mosque. His popularity increases. He meets many Maghrebīs, disputes with some of the disciples of Ibn Sabᶜīn and of Ibn ᶜArabī – and leads some of them (among them somebody close to al-Manbijī) back to the straight path. He composes a first version of his *al-Radd ᶜalā l-manṭiqiyyīn* ('Refutation of the logicians').

In Damascus, Baybars also takes some measures against several friends of Ibn Taymiyya.

The release of Ibn Taymiyya intervenes on the occasion of the return to power of the sultan al-Nāṣir, and on his order.

709/1310, 2 Shawwāl/5 March:

Baybars al-Jāshnikīr having been forced to abdicate, al-Nāṣir begins his third reign, which will last until 741/1341, and mark the apogee of the Mamlūk regime. He will have Baybars strangled in Dhū l-Qaʿda 709/April 1310 and, a little later, the emir Salār starved to death.

709/1310:

The īlkhān Öljāytū converts to Shīʿism and commits himself to a policy resolutely opposed to Sunnism.

709/1310, 8 Shawwāl/11 March:

Return of Ibn Taymiyya to Cairo, where he settles for about three years in the al-Ḥusayn quarter. Almost immediately granted an audience by al-Nāṣir, he persuades him to maintain the statute imposed on the *dhimmī*s by Baybars al-Jāshnikīr. He receives many visitors, teaches in the mosques or at diverse gatherings, and gives fatwas. His popularity and influence are very great.

A sort of *éminence grise* or minister-without-portfolio for al-Nāṣir, Ibn Taymiyya is at times consulted by him or takes the initiative to give him counsel, notably on his religious–legal duties of governance or on Syrian affairs. He begins his *Kitāb al-Siyāsat al-sharʿiyya* ('The book of religious–legal governance'), which he will complete after his return to Damascus.

711/1311, 4 Rajab/16 November:

While praying alone in al-Ḥākim mosque, Ibn Taymiyya is beaten up by a group of people. Found by his companions and the people of the al-Ḥusayn quarter, he has to work strenuously to persuade them not to massacre his assailants and destroy their houses. Returning the same afternoon to pray in al-Ḥākim mosque, he preaches until the evening and wins over a party of his enemies.

711/311, middle Rajab/end November:

Ibn Taymiyya is assaulted by the Shāfiʿī shaykh Nūr al-Dīn al-Bakrī (d. 724/1324), the very same whom he attacks fiercely on the subject of the worship of saints in his book

Kitāb al-Istighātha ('The book of appealing for help'), also titled *al-Radd ʿalā l-Bakrī* ('The refutation of al-Bakrī'). Al-Bakrī wishes to drag him before the tribunal but then soon disappears in the crowd. A near riot ensues; Ibn Taymiyya has to prevent his supporters from taking revenge on al-Bakrī.

712/1312:

Composition of *al-Qāʿidat al-Marrākushiyya* ('The Marrakeshi ruling') on the divine attributes and God's sitting on the Throne. As soon as it reaches the Maghreb, this fatwa will contribute greatly to the renown of the Shaykh al-Islām.

Composition of Ibn Taymiyya's *Sharḥ al-ʿaqīdat al-Iṣfahāniyya* – 'Commentary on the creed of Shams al-Dīn al-Iṣfahānī', a disciple of Fakhr al-Dīn al-Rāzī (d. 749/1349). To this period may be dated the Shaykh al-Islām's *al-Jawāb al-ṣaḥīḥ li-man baddala dīn al-Masīḥ* ('The correct response to those who have replaced the religion of the Messiah'). Ibn Taymiyya himself explains that he wrote it in response to a letter from the Nazarenes requesting it, and after he had written 'a commentary on the *Creed* composed by the Shaykh Shams al-Dīn al-Iṣfahānī' (IBN TAYMIYYA, *Kitāb al-Nubuwwāt*).

712/1313, 1 Dhū l-Qaʿda/ 27 February:

The arrival of Ibn Taymiyya, his two brothers, and some disciples, in Damascus, where he is welcomed with joyous parade. He left Cairo with the sultan and the Egyptian army, following the threat of a new Mongol invasion of Syria, perhaps instigated by emirs gone over to the Mongols' side, among them the former governor of Damascus, al-Afram, and the Bedouin chief Muhannā b. ʿĪsā. The Tatars giving up the project, Ibn Taymiyya left the army at Ghazza and stopped for some time in Jerusalem. He will not leave Damascus again until his death.

It is apparently in reference to this threat of invasion that Ibn Taymiyya writes the longest of his three anti-Mongol fatwas. (Long extracts from these are translated in MICHOT, 'Textes spirituels XI–XIII'.)

He resumes teaching at the Sukkariyya and the Ḥanbaliyya and devotes himself to knowledge. He is promoted to the rank of head of school and considered by his partisans as an independent *mujtahid.* He writes a great deal and gives many fatwas, conforming or not conforming to the four traditionnal rites – which will be the principal reason for his troubles during this period.

713/1313:

Ibn Qayyim al-Jawziyya (691–751/1292–1350) attaches himself to Ibn Taymiyya. The latter has numerous other partisans, disciples and faithful supporters, among the emirs, as also among the womenfolk of Damascus. However, he seems not to have been appreciated by the new governor of the city, the emir Sayf al-Dīn Tankiz (d. 741/1241), to say nothing of the Shāfiʿī chief qāḍī, still in office, Ibn Ṣaṣrā.

It is apparently during the years following (713–17/1313–17) that, according to its editor, M. Sālim, Ibn Taymiyya composes his magisterial *Darʾ taʿāruḍ al-ʿaql wa-l-naql* ('Rejection of the contradiction between reason and tradition'), wherein he comments at length on Avicenna, al-Suhrawardī, al-Ghazālī, Abū l-Barakāt al-Baghdādī, Fakhr al-Dīn al-Rāzī, and others. Passages are translated in MICHOT, 'Vanités intellectuelles', and 'A Mamlūk Theologian's Commentary on Avicenna... I and II'.

716/1317, 20 Shawwāl/5 January:

Death of Ibn Taymiyya's mother. (A letter of Ibn Taymiyya to his mother is translated in MICHOT, 'Un célibataire endurci...')

716/1317, Dhū l-Qaʿda/January:

Death of Öljāytū. Enthronement of the īlkhān Abū Saʿīd (d. 736/1335), who reverts to Sunnism.

717/1317:

Ibn Taymiyya is consulted by the Bedouin emir Muhannā b. ʿĪsā, recently returned from the Tatar to the Mamlūk camp. The sultan also consults Ibn Taymiyya – about the goods taken by the same Muhannā b. ʿĪsā at the time of his victory over the Shīʿī emir al-Dalaqnadī (who was allied to the pro-

Shī'ī and pro-Mongol emir of Makka, Ḥumayḍa) just before his (Muhannā's) return from the Mongols' side. The goods are to be the price of his rehabilitation in Cairo.

While his brother Sharaf al-Dīn is on pilgrimage, the Shaykh al-Islām takes his courses at the madrasa Ḥanbaliyya.

Ibn Taymiyya's fatwa against the Nuṣayrīs may date from this period, during which the sultan al-Nāṣir leads an active anti-Shī'ī policy, notably against the Rāfiḍīs of the Syrian–Lebanese mountains and coast.

718/1318, 27 Rabīᶜ I/10 May:

Ibn Taymiyya signs an *ijāza* on a short epistle on the oath of repudiation – *al-Ijtimāᶜ wa-l-iftirāq fī l-ḥilf bi-l-ṭalāq* ('Reunion and separation concerning the oath on pain of divorce') – which he has just completed. During the following months this epistle will be rejected by the chief Shāfi'ī qāḍī of Egypt, Taqī l-Dīn al-Subkī (d. 756/1355). (See Y. RAPOPORT, *Marriage, Money and Divorce in Medieval Islamic Society* (2005), 96.)

718/1318, 15 Rabīᶜ II/15 June:

On the advice of some eminent muftis of Damascus, Shams al-Dīn b. Muslim (d. 726/1326), Ḥanbalī chief qāḍī, recommends to Ibn Taymiyya that he no longer give fatwas on the question of the oath on pain of divorce. Ibn Taymiyya accepts his reasons.

718/1318, 1 Jumādā I/30 June:

Arrival in Damascus of a letter from the sultan al-Nāṣir forbidding Ibn Taymiyya to give fatwas on the oath on pain of divorce and ordering the holding of a council on the subject. This council takes place two days later, endorses the sultan's letter and has it proclaimed in the city. Nevertheless, Ibn Taymiyya, invoking the religious–legal prohibition against hiding knowledge, will continue to give fatwas on the matter.

719/1319, 29 Ramaḍān/13 November:

During a council of the qāḍīs and principal jurists before the governor Tankiz, the letter of the sultan al-Nāṣir is read out in order to remind Ibn Taymiyya of the interdiction against giving fatwas on repudiation. Ibn Taymiyya will ignore it.

720–21/1320–21, 22 Rajab–10 Muḥarram/27 August–8 Feb.:
Detention of Ibn Taymiyya in the citadel of Damascus, following the condemnation of him at a new council of qāḍīs and muftis before Tankiz: during it he is reproached for persisting in giving fatwas on the question of repudiation. He will be released by a decree of al-Nāṣir and resume his teaching and other activities.

721/1321:
Violent discord explodes between Christians and Muslims in Cairo, with burning of churches and mosques.
During the years that follow, perhaps at the request of the Mamlūk power, Ibn Taymiyya composes *Minhāj al-sunnat al-nabawiyya* ('The way of the Prophet's *Sunna*'), a refutation of *Minhāj al-karāma* ('The way of charisma'), put into writing in 721/1321 by the great Shīʿī theologian al-Muṭahhar al-Ḥillī (d. 726/1325). According to Henri Laoust, the *Ḥisba* might also be dated to this period.
One may also with good reason place within the years 720–26/1320–26 the composition of his *Risāla ilā Abī l-Fiḍāʾ* ('Letter to Abū l-Fiḍāʾ', translated in MICHOT, *Lettre à Abū l-Fidāʾ*).

725/1325, 12 Shawwāl/21 September:
A lively argument ensues between Ibn Taymiyya and shaykh Shams al-Dīn Maḥmūd al-Iṣfahānī, on the occasion of his inaugural lesson at the madrasa Rawāḥiyya. Having arrived in Damascus at the beginning of the year, Shaykh al-Iṣfahānī had nevertheless been assiduous in seeking out the company of Ibn Taymiyya, who had written for him his *Sharḥ al-ʿAqīdat al-Isfahāniyya* ('Commentary on the Creed of Iṣpahān').

726/1326, 21 Rabīʿ I/25 February:
At the occasion of the public execution of the atheist Nāṣir al-Dīn b. al-Sharaf b. al-Ḥaythī, Ibn Taymiyya detaches himself from the crowd and goes to strike the condemned man with his hand.

726/1326, 6 Shaʿbān/7 July:

Ibn Taymiyya is arrested on the order of the sultan al-Nāṣir and the instruction of Tankiz – the sequel of a long-running case targeting his ideas about visiting graves, among them the Prophet's grave in Madina, something that he is accused of having considered to be proscribed by consensus (*ijmāʿ*).

The arrest takes place on Monday 6th, not 'Monday 16th' – as Ibn Kathīr and numerous authors following him have written. In fact the 16th was a Thursday.

A former fatwa on the subject by the Shaykh al-Islām has been discovered by a group of people and has given rise to controversies and tittle-tattle. With intrigues, calumnies and the distortion of his ideas helping, the case has rapidly acquired the proportions of a scandal, the more dangerous as his companions do not always stay calm. In Damascus certain people have considered exiling Ibn Taymiyya, of cutting out his tongue, of imprisoning him, etc. In Cairo, a fatwa by the Mālikī chief qāḍī, Taqī l-Dīn al-Ikhnāʾī (d. 750/ 1349), and others has declared him an unbeliever. A death sentence is demanded of the sultan al-Nāṣir, who refuses and reconvenes the chief qāḍīs. It is after their verdict that the sultan has the Shaykh al-Islām imprisoned – without any other form of trial, without allowing him the opportunity to defend himself.

Happy to have been arrested, Ibn Taymiyya allows himself to be led away, without resistance, to the citadel of Damascus, where he will remain in detention until his death. He is given a spacious room supplied with water. His brother Zayn al-Dīn gets from the sultan permission to stay with him in order to serve him, and money with which to cover his needs.

726/1326, 10 Shaʿbān/11 July:

A letter from the sultan is read out in the Umayyad Mosque. It commands the imprisonment of Ibn Taymiyya and withdraws from him the right to give fatwas.

726/1326, 15 Shaʿbān/16 July:

With the permission of Tankiz, the Shāfiʿī chief qāḍī of Damascus, Jalāl al-Dīn al-Qazwīnī, has a number of Ibn Taymiyya's disciples imprisoned. Several will be paraded on donkeys and publicly denounced, then released. After having been thus exhibited and whipped, Ibn Qayyim al-Jawziyya is imprisoned in the citadel with Ibn Taymiyya and will not be freed until after the death of his master.

726/1326, 7 Ramaḍān/6 August:

On this Thursday Ibn Baṭṭūta arrives in Damascus, proceeding from Cairo. His memory of this date is faulty or, quite simply, he is inventing when, in his travel account, he claims to have attended a Friday sermon given by Ibn Taymiyya. In fact Ibn Taymiyya had been detained in the citadel for a month past. The rest of the great Maghrebī traveller's account of the Shaykh al-Islām, vaguely inspired by his trials of 705–07/1306–07, is not much more credible.

726/1326, 10 Dhū l-Qaʿda/7 October:

Burhān al-Dīn b. Hilāl al-Zurʿī resumes Ibn Taymiyya's courses at the madrasa Ḥanbaliyya.

726/1326, 11 Dhū l-Qaʿda/8 October:

Ibn Taymiyya is interrogated in prison, by the Shāfiʿī qāḍī Jamal al-Dīn b. Jumla (d. 738/1338), on his *Risāla fī ziyārat al-qubūr* ('Letter on visiting graves'). The point of view that he expounds, though set in writing, is knowingly distorted by Ibn Jumla.

727/1327:

ʿAlāʾ al-Dīn al-Qūnawī (d. 729/1329), disciple of Ibn ʿArabī and superior of the mystics of Cairo, is named as the new Shāfiʿī chief qāḍī in Damascus. Before his departure for Syria, he is charged by the sultan al-Nāṣir to intervene with Tankiz to secure the release of Ibn Taymiyya. The project remained unrealized.

In his prison, Ibn Taymiyya continues to write and to give fatwas. Notably, he composes *Kitāb Maʿārij al-wuṣūl ilā maʿrifat anna uṣūl al-dīn wa-furūʿa-hu qad bayyana-hā l-rasūl* ('Book of the Degrees of attainment of the knowledge that the fundamentals of the religion and their derived branches, were fully expounded by the Messenger'), and *Rafᶜ al-malām ᶜan al-aʾimmat al-aᶜlām* ('Lifting the blame from the most eminent of the imāms').

In addition, on the subject of visiting graves Ibn Taymiyya conducts a fierce polemic against Taqī al-Dīn al-Ikhnāʾī, who has attempted to refute his views on the question and has, on the same matter, had one of his disciples, Shihāb al-Dīn b. Murrī, condemned in Cairo. He writes his very harsh *Kitāb al-Radd ᶜalā l-Ikhnāʾī* ('Book on the Refutation of al-Ikhnāʾī').

727/1327, 14 Jumāda I/7 April:
Death of Ibn Taymiyya's brother, Sharaf al-Dīn.

728/1328, 9 Jumāda II/21 April:
By an order of the sultan, instigated by a complaint of al-Ikhnāʾī, Ibn Taymiyya's books, papers, ink and pens are withdrawn from him. He will dedicate the last months of his life to worship, and write his last words with a bit of charcoal.

728/1328, 1 Rajab/12 May:
Ibn Taymiyya's books are transported to the library of the great madrasa ᶜĀdiliyya. The qāḍīs and jurists examine them, then divide them among themselves.

728/1328, 20 Dhū l-Qaᶜda/25 September:
Ibn Taymiyya dies in his prison, in the citadel of Damascus. He has been ill for the past three weeks. The populace of Damascus crowd his funeral, among them many women – the Shaykh al-Islām, as we know, never married. He is buried in the Cemetery of the Sufis, beside his brother, Sharaf al-Dīn. (For an account of his funeral, the fate of that cemetery, and the current neglect of the great man's tomb, see MICHOT, *Pour une tombe*.)

INDEXES

Page numbers shown in **bold** indicate occurrences within passages of Ibn Taymiyya.

QUR'ĀNIC VERSES

ḤADĪTHS OF THE PROPHET

TEXTS OF IBN TAYMIYYA TRANSLATED

OTHER ARABIC AND PERSIAN TEXTS TRANSLATED

GEOGRAPHICAL TERMS

PERSONS, GROUPS, DOCTRINES

KEYWORDS AND CONCEPTS

TRANSCRIBED WORDS